Why Do You Need This New Edition?

If you're wondering why you should buy this new edition of *Reading Rhetorically*, here are a few great reasons!

1. Each chapter now opens with a list of learning objectives. These objectives state what topics you should have mastered after studying the chapter.

2. New readings provide you with useful models for how to read rhetorically across a variety of genres (Chapters 2 and 3).

3. New, thought-provoking visuals have been added throughout that will promote class discussion and analysis.

4. Streamlined discussion of visual arguments will help prepare you for engaging with similar materials found on the Web (Chapter 4).

5. Visual texts receive increased emphasis throughout the book, from visual arguments in Chapters 1 and 4 to new citation models in the Appendix.

6. Reorganized table of rhetorical aims ("A Spectrum of Purposes") highlights a variety of undergraduate writing assignments across the curriculum (Chapter 2).

7. Boxed features concisely provide advice on such topics as analyzing an author's purpose and exploring your own responses to a text (Chapters 3 and 4).

8. The MLA formatting guidelines have been updated with more examples of citing digital sources (Chapter 6 and Appendix).

PEARSON

Reading Rhetorically

Fourth Edition

JOHN C. BEAN
Seattle University

VIRGINIA A. CHAPPELL
Marquette University

ALICE M. GILLAM
University of Wisconsin–Milwaukee

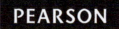

Boston   Columbus   Indianapolis   New York   San Francisco   Upper Saddle River
Amsterdam   Cape Town   Dubai   London   Madrid   Milan   Munich   Paris   Montreal   Toronto
Delhi   Mexico City   São Paulo   Sydney   Hong Kong   Seoul   Singapore   Taipei   Tokyo

Senior Sponsoring Editor: Katharine Glynn
Senior Marketing Manager: Sandra McGuire
Executive Digital Producer: Stefanie A. Snajder
Production Manager: Laura Messerly
Project Coordination and Electronic Page Makeup: Shyam Ramasubramony, S4Carlisle
  Publishing Services
Senior Art Director: Jayne Conte
Cover Designer/Manager: Suzanne Behnke
Cover Art: Shutterstock
Printer/Binder: LSC Communications
Cover Printer: Lehigh/Phoenix

Credits and acknowledgments for materials borrowed from other sources
and reproduced, with permission, in this text appear on pages 173-174.

Library of Congress Cataloging-in-Publication Data

Bean, John C.
  Reading rhetorically / John C. Bean, Seattle University, Virginia A. Chappell,
Marquette University, Alice M. Gillam, University of Wisconsin-Milwaukee. —
Fourth edition.
    pages cm
Includes bibliographical references.
ISBN-13: 978-0-321-84662-4 (Student ISBN)
ISBN-10: 0-321-84662-1 (Student ISBN)
  1. College readers.   2. English language—Rhetoric—Problems, exercises, etc.
3. Report writing—Problems, exercises, etc.   I. Chappell, Virginia A.   II. Gillam,
Alice M.   III. Title.
  PE1417.B393 2012
  808'.0427—dc23

                                                                    2012047604

Student ISBN 10:   0-321-84662-1
Student ISBN 13: 978-0-321-84662-4

Contents

Preface

The students we are meeting in our composition courses are disturbingly eager to grab information quickly off a screen or page, without pausing to consider its purpose or usefulness to their purposes. As new forms of media proliferate and as the lines between information and entertainment blur, critical reading and rhetorical analysis become even more important components of college composition courses. Accordingly, this fourth edition of *Reading Rhetorically* provides explicit instruction in those crucial skills. It is grounded in our conviction that freshly sharpened reading skills will help college students not only write more substantial papers than otherwise but also engage with both the academic and public spheres on more sophisticated and productive terms. To paraphrase Aristotle, "Everyone uses rhetoric but those who understand it can control those who do not." We have designed the book to help students understand rhetoric and thus to be critical readers and writers of the word and of the world.

Reading Rhetorically has been adopted at many different instructional levels at a range of two- and four-year institutions for use in a variety of classrooms—including entry-level courses, upper-level writing courses, AP and college-prep writing courses, and even faculty development seminars—all confirming our belief that academic reading, writing, and inquiry need to be taught as inextricably linked rhetorical acts. Recommendations from faculty who have taught with the book have helped us choose new readings for this edition and include visual elements to help students grasp content quickly. At the same time, we have preserved the primary identity of *Reading Rhetorically* as an aims-based composition text that (1) emphasizes reading as an interactive process of composing meaning and (2) treats academic writing as a process in which writers engage with other texts.

This textbook teaches students to read with an analytical eye and to write about what they have read with rhetorical insight. We define "reading rhetorically" as attending to an author's purposes for writing and to the methods the author uses to accomplish those purposes—the *how* as well as the *what* of a text's message. By introducing the concept of *ethos*, the book takes students beyond the *logos* of a text's argument to examine how the text projects its author's qualifications and motives. By introducing the concept of *pathos*, the book focuses students on how a text endeavors to engage an audience's interests and emotions. It connects the *activity* of meaning-making—reading and writing—to the *study* of meaning-making. In other words, the book teaches students

- How to see texts as positioned in a conversation with other texts
- How to recognize the rhetorical aims and persuasive strategies of a given text
- How to analyze a text for both content and rhetorical method

Students who use *Reading Rhetorically* hone their analytical skills and learn to write with rhetorical sophistication. They practice analyzing texts by reading them with and against the grain; they learn to imitate the rhetorical strategies and genre conventions manifest in the texts they study; and they apply these analytical techniques for their own purposes when they conduct research. Our overall goal is to offer techniques for rhetorical analysis so that students can learn about, then apply in their own writing, a variety of rhetorical strategies.

What's New in the Fourth Edition

- Each chapter now opens with a list of learning objectives that clearly state what topics each student should have mastered after studying the chapter.
- New readings provide students with useful and engaging models for applying newly learned strategies for reading rhetorically across a variety of genres.
- New, thought-provoking visuals have been added throughout that will promote class discussion and analysis.
- Streamlined discussion of visual arguments will help prepare students for engaging with similar materials on the Web.
- Throughout, visual texts receive increased emphasis, from visual arguments in Chapters 1 and 4 to new citation models in the Appendix.
- The reorganized table of rhetorical aims ("A Spectrum of Purposes") in Chapter 2 highlights a variety of undergraduate writing assignments across the curriculum.
- Boxed features concisely provide advice on such topics as analyzing an author's purpose and exploring your own responses to a text.
- The MLA formatting guidelines have been updated with more examples for citing visual and digital sources.

Distinctive Features

The fourth edition of *Reading Rhetorically* is distinguished by the following features:

- **Its emphasis on academic writing** as a process in which writers engage with other texts
- **Assignments** that emphasize strategies for writing *about* reading
- **An emphasis on reading as an interactive process** of composing meaning
- **Well-integrated "For Writing and Discussion"** activities that foster active learning by asking students to apply concepts immediately
- **An analytical framework** for understanding and critiquing how visual texts interact with verbal texts

- **Treatment of rhetorical analysis** both as an academic genre that sharpens students' reading acuity and as a tool for academic research
- **Explanations of classical rhetorical concepts** as they apply to reading and critiquing both verbal and visual texts
- **Graphic presentation of composing processes** from invention through peer review to editing
- **Treatment of research as a process of rhetorical reading** in which students learn to develop research questions and evaluate sources within a rhetorical context
- **Emphasis on Question Analysis** as a technique for planning research, with extensive excerpts from a sample student research log
- **A thorough discussion of how to evaluate sources**, including Web sources and licensed periodicals databases
- **Presentation of citation methods** as integral to rhetorical effectiveness
- **Model citations** for print and electronic materials in the 2009 MLA format

Structure

The fourth edition's organization, which continues the structure established in the third edition, introduces key concepts about both reading and writing in Chapter 1, which explains how rhetorical reading can empower student writers. Chapter 2 elaborates on this concept by introducing the concept of the *rhetorical situation* and showing students how to use rhetorical knowledge to read more efficiently. Chapters 3 and 4 provide details about *how* to read rhetorically, first by "listening" to what a text is doing and saying, and second by questioning what a text is doing and saying. Chapter 3 offers practice in listening through annotating, mapping idea structure, taking a text's visual features into account, summarizing, descriptive outlining, and writing a rhetorical précis. Chapter 4 provides practice in questioning texts through analysis of rhetorical appeals, language, and ideology, offering extensive coverage of the rhetorical impact of visuals. Throughout, we provide sample texts based on student writing about short readings placed at the end of Chapters 2– 4: a brief report about research on gum-chewing from the *UC Berkeley Wellness Letter*, a commentary from art critic Kirk Savage about the Vietnam Veterans Memorial (excerpted from his book *Monument Wars*), and a *New York Times* op-ed piece about medical checklists by surgeon Atul Gawande. The Savage book is also the basis of an extended example illustrating how to use spot reading to evaluate the potential value of a book-length research source.

Chapters 5 and 6 then focus on specific analytic techniques for (a) using rhetorical reading to conduct research and (b) incorporating material from sources into academic papers. These chapters detail specific guidelines to help students work with summaries, paraphrases, direct quotations, and citations within a rhetorical framework. Finally, the appendix, which is readily accessible from any chapter, provides easy-to-follow models for MLA-style citations.

Strategies for Using *Reading Rhetorically*

The text's organizational structure facilitates easy syllabus design by providing a conceptual framework and practical strategies for reading and writing about a broad range of texts. Students can work their way through these chapters before proceeding to course readings, or they can move back and forth between this text and course readings, trying out various reading and writing strategies as they develop papers from assigned texts.

Supplements

Instructor's Manual

The online *Instructor's Resource Manual* will help both new and experienced instructors make curricular decisions and plan daily classroom activities. Easy to search, it is designed to facilitate efficient planning and offers numerous suggestions and links for extending discussion in the book to materials found on Web sites. The manual demonstrates the book's flexibility by (1) showing how to integrate instruction in rhetorical analysis with a variety of reading and writing assignments, (2) describing classroom activities that encourage students to apply their rhetorical reading skills, (3) presenting additional writing assignments, and (4) outlining the connections between *Reading Rhetorically* and the Council of Writing Program Administrators' *Outcomes Statement*. These teaching suggestions are all adaptable according to a variety of curricular goals, whether the focus is on, for example, academic writing, introducing students to a variety of rhetorical aims, or persuasion and writing for the public sphere.

Pearson MyLab

Students can use their Pearson MyLab on their own, benefiting from self-paced diagnostics and a personal learning path that recommends the instruction and practice each student needs to improve his or her writing skills. Your Pearson MyLab is an eminently flexible application that instructors can use in ways that best complement their courses and teaching styles. They can recommend it to students for self-study, track student progress, or leverage the power of administrative features to be more effective and save time. The assignment builder and commenting tools, developed specifically for writing instruction, bring instructors closer to their student writers, make managing assignments and evaluating papers more efficient, and put powerful assessment within reach. Students receive feedback within the context of their own writing, which encourages critical thinking and revision and helps them to develop skills based on their individual needs.

Learn more at www.PearsonMyLab.com.

Acknowledgments

We begin by thanking the teachers who have used the third edition of *Reading Rhetorically* and offered excellent advice for the fourth edition:

Dianna Baldwin, Michigan State University
Patricia Gillikin, University of New Mexico, Valencia
Jeanne Guerin, California State University, Sacramento
Jeff Tate, Northern Oklahoma College
Stephanie Vie, Fort Lewis College

Our thanks go to colleagues and students (past and present) whose ideas and feedback have been invaluable to this book through four editions, especially the leaders and participants in the Cal State Early Assessment Program and Expository Reading and Writing Course, whose imaginative and inspired use of *Reading Rhetorically* has, in turn, inspired us: Nancy Brynelson, Roberta Ching, John Edlund, Kim Flachmann, Mary Kay Harrington, Mira-Lisa Katz, Alison Warriner, and the many high school teachers whose innovative assignment modules have demonstrated the power of rhetorical concepts for guiding students to success. More personally, we thank Marquette students Neal Gregus and Alex Koepsel for a particularly productive brainstorming session at Starbucks, and our families for ongoing support and patience with our deadlines.

To our editor at Pearson Longman, Katharine Glynn, we offer many thanks for guidance, patience, and grace under pressure. In addition, we send continuing gratitude to Lauren Finn, who guided us through the second and third editions, lending her creativity to the graphics in Chapter 6. We also wish to acknowledge again the skill and insight of our first editor, Eben Ludlow, and the amazing problem-solving ability of development editor Marion Castellucci, who worked on the second edition, from whom we learned how to prepare manuscripts for publication.

Finally, we thank all our students over the years, including writers at all levels, teachers-in-training, and graduate assistants. In writing centers, classrooms, and office conferences, we have learned from them how to bring together rhetorical theory and practice in ways that foster astute reading and effective writing. We have said it before, and the truth endures: We learn from every paper we grade, every student with whom we discuss a draft. For the trust that students place in us and for the opportunity to watch them learn and grow as writers, we are profoundly grateful.

John C. Bean
Virginia A. Chappell
Alice M. Gillam

CHAPTER 1

Reading to Write: Strategies for College Writing

Academic writing, reading, and inquiry are inseparably linked; and all three are learned by not doing any one alone, but by doing them all at the same time.

—James Reither

We have designed this book to help you succeed at the writing, reading, and inquiry tasks that James Reither refers to above. College students are often surprised, even overwhelmed, by the heavy reading they are assigned and by the challenge of integrating material from that reading in their own writing. Along with textbook chapters and other assigned readings in a course, your college reading will include specialized Web sites, books, articles, and abstracts that you will examine in order to prepare research papers for a wide variety of classes, not only for English but for natural science, social science, and pre-professional classes such as introductory courses in accounting or nursing. Throughout this book, we will be describing and explaining how the techniques of **reading rhetorically** will help you do all this successfully.

In this chapter, you will learn:

- How strategies for "reading rhetorically" can enhance your academic success
- How the metaphors of "conversation" and "composing" can deepen your understanding of your reading processes
- How eight key questions for reading rhetorically can help you analyze a text

Imagine the following scenario: It's early evening on Thursday, and you are planning your weekend's study schedule. Besides an assignment to read a chapter in your chemistry textbook for Monday, you have some writing assignments due next week. Consider this hypothetical list of reading and writing assignments that you need to get started on over the weekend:

- Find and analyze a local newspaper editorial for your political science class according to concepts laid out in a textbook chapter titled "Interest Groups and the Media."
- Summarize and write a critical reflection on a recent *Atlantic* online Web "Dispatch" assigned for your Environmental Studies class.
- Identify points of difficulty in a Platonic dialogue for your humanities seminar and formulate questions about them for discussion.
- Begin developing a research question for a major paper for your African history class, due next month.

For many students, a list like this seems daunting simply because it lays out many different kinds of reading and writing tasks that all must be done in the same relatively short period of time. This challenge of what some people call "allatonceness" is what this book is designed to help you with. The techniques of reading rhetorically—the central concept of this book—will help you sort through and develop the varied reading and writing skills called for in college courses.

For each assignment on our hypothetical list, your ability to meet your instructor's goals would depend not only on your ability to craft clear, grammatical sentences, but also on your ability to read insightfully and analytically. Note that each one calls upon students to read in a particular way. This variety occurs because professors design assignments to help students learn not just the subject matter but the academic methods central to their disciplines. Thus, assignments often necessitate reading with different purposes and types of awareness. In these four cases, students need to

- Comprehend political science textbook concepts about interest groups well enough to tie them to an editorial
- Distill the key ideas in a popular Web article and reflect upon how they apply (or not) to ideas being discussed in a course
- Spot ambiguities and formulate discussion questions that zero in on them
- Scan through class notes and library databases to locate issues that will focus on an individual research question

For the most part, students adapt to these new demands and gradually learn what academic reading entails, so that by the time they are juniors and seniors within their major fields, they know how to do the reading and writing demanded in their disciplines and future professions. But the process is often slow and frustrating, marked by trial and error and the panicky feeling that reading for different purposes is like hacking through a jungle when there might be a path nearby that could make the journey easier.

We hope that learning to read rhetorically, a concept that informs every chapter of this book, will help you find that path and thus accelerate your growth as a strong academic reader and writer.

What Do We Mean by "Reading Rhetorically"?

To read rhetorically is (1) to read with attention to how your purposes for read- ing may or may not match an author's purposes for writing and (2) to recognize the methods that authors use to try to accomplish their purposes. Remember this: All authors have designs on their readers. Authors want their readers to see things their way so that readers will adopt their point of view. But rhetorical readers know how to maintain a critical distance from a text and thus determine carefully the extent to which they will go along with the author.

As you move into your college majors, new writing assignments will ask you to write about your reading in a way that shows that you are "doing" a discipline, for example, *doing* political science or *doing* philosophy. That is why we stress throughout these chapters the importance of interacting with a text beyond just understanding what it says. In college, reporting about what you have read will be only a beginning point. You will be asked to find meaning, not merely information, in books and articles. You will be asked to respond to that meaning—to explain it, to use it, to analyze it, to critique it, to compare it to alternative meanings that other writers have created or that you create yourself as you write.

To fulfill such writing and reading assignments, you will need to analyze not just *what* texts say but *how* they say it. This double awareness is crucial to reading rhetorically. By analyzing both the content and the technique of a given text, a rhetorical reader critically considers the extent to which he or she will accept or question that text.

The Demands and Pleasures of Academic Reading

Once you become immersed in academic life—caught up in the challenge of doing your own questioning, critical thinking, analysis, and research—you'll discover that academic reading has unique demands and pleasures. If you ask an experienced academic reader engaged in a research project why she reads, her answer may be something like this: "I'm investigating a problem that re- quires close analysis of several primary sources. I also need to read secondary sources to see what other researchers are saying about this problem. Then I can position myself in the conversation."

This may seem a curious answer—one that you might not fully under- stand until you have had more experience writing papers that require analysis or research. To help you appreciate this answer—and to see how it applies to you—consider that in most college courses, you will have two underlying goals:

Goal 1. Learning conceptual knowledge. You need to learn the body of information presented in the course—to master the key concepts and ideas of the course, to memorize important facts, to learn key definitions or formulas, to understand the discipline's theories, and understand how they seek to explain certain data and observations. Cognitive psychologists sometimes call this kind of learning **conceptual knowledge**—that is, knowledge of the course's subject matter. Transmitting conceptual knowledge is the primary aim of most college textbooks. Ironically, even textbooks designed for beginners present challenging reading assignments because their pages are packed with specialized terminology that students need to know if they are to follow lectures, pass exams, and, more generally, understand how chemists (for example) think about, label, and measure the physical world.

Goal 2. Learning procedural knowledge. Most college courses are designed to help you learn the discipline's characteristic ways of applying conceptual knowledge to new problems. What questions does the discipline ask? What are its methods of analysis or research? What counts as evidence? What are the discipline's shared or disputed assumptions? How do you write arguments in this discipline, and what makes them convincing (say in literature, sociology, engineering, or accounting)? Thus, in addition to learning the basic concepts of a course, you need to learn how experts in the discipline pose problems and conduct inquiry. Cognitive psychologists call this kind of learning **procedural knowledge**—the ability to apply conceptual knowledge to new problems by using the discipline's characteristic methods of thinking.

When teachers assign readings beyond the typical textbook—newspaper or magazine articles, scholarly articles, or primary sources such as historical documents or literary texts—they are asking you to use procedural knowledge by analyzing or using these readings in discipline-specific ways. Consider the political science assignment in our opening scenario. The professor who assigned analysis of a local newspaper editorial undoubtedly wants students to learn what the textbook says about interest-group politics (conceptual knowledge), and then to apply those concepts to analyze current events (procedural knowledge). As you read a variety of editorials looking for one to analyze, you would need to read them through the lens of your political science textbook. A different kind of challenge is presented by the Platonic dialogue. Not only does it contain complex ideas, but it also demonstrates a form of discourse and a philosophical way of thinking that has had a lasting impact on European traditions. The professor's decision to start by asking students to raise questions about difficult passages provides a way for students to start exploring the text without being intimidated by it.

As you read the various kinds of texts assigned in your courses and write different kinds of papers, you will discover that academic disciplines are not inert bodies of knowledge but contested fields full of uncertainties, disagreements, and debate. You will see why college professors want you to *do* their discipline rather than simply study it. They want you not just to study chemistry or political science or history, but to *think like a chemist or a political scientist or an historian.* As you learn to read rhetorically, you will learn to recognize different authors' purposes and methods, the ways that claims are typically asserted and supported in different disciplines, and the types of evidence that are valued by those disciplines. For example, historians value primary sources such as letters and diaries, government records, and legal documents. Psychologists gather quite different kinds of research data, such as empirical observations of an animal's learning behaviors under different diet conditions, statistical data about the reduction of anxiety symptoms in humans after different kinds of therapy, or "think-aloud" transcripts of a person's problem-solving processes after varying amounts of sleep. Your accumulating knowledge about disciplinary discourses will teach you new ways of thinking, and you will learn to use those methods in your own writing.

It is important to realize that even people with considerable background knowledge and high interest in a subject will probably find course readings daunting when they are dense with new concepts, vocabulary, and information. With so much unfamiliar material, each new sentence can seem just as important as the one before, causing you to think, "I've got to know all of this—how will I ever write anything about it?" Reading rhetorically can help you separate key concepts from supporting details.

Reading and Writing as Conversation

Consider again how our experienced researcher at the beginning of the last section answered the question, "Why do you read?" It is obvious that she is immersed in *doing* her discipline and that she sees reading as central to her work. But she also says that she is reading "to position myself in the conversation." What does she mean by that? How is reading part of a "conversation"?

To understand this metaphor of conversation, think of writers as talking to readers—and think of readers as talking back. For example, suppose our researcher's investigation leads her to new insights that she would like to share with others. If she is a professional scholar, she may write an academic article. If she is an undergraduate, she may write a research paper. In both cases, her intended audience would be academic readers interested in a particular problem or question. Motivated by the belief that she has produced something new or controversial to add to the conversation, she aims to present the results of her research and try to persuade readers to accept her argument and claims.

Thinking of yourself as joining a conversation will be helpful whenever you read or write so that you can consider not only the text you are reading, but also the conversation that it joins. Think of this conversation as multi-voiced. The first voice is that of the text's author; a second voice (actually a set of voices) is the network of other writers the author refers to—previous participants in the conversation. The third voice is yours as you respond to the text while you read, and later when you write something about it.

This broad view of readers and writers interacting via texts extends the metaphor of "conversation" to say that texts themselves are in a conversation with previous texts. Each text acts in relationship to other texts. It asserts a claim on a reader's attention by invoking certain interests and understandings, reminding readers of what has been previously written about the subject. For example, articles in scientific journals typically begin with a **literature review**; that is, a summary of important research already conducted on the question at hand. Similarly, political commentators will summarize the views of others so that they can affirm, extend, or take issue with those views. In the arts, reviewers of music, film, and books are likely to refer to (and, on the Web, perhaps link to) not just the work under review but discussions about the given artist's reputation, which, of course, was established not just by word of mouth but also by other texts or performances with which the current reader may not be familiar.

Joining the Conversation

The reasons any of us engage in conversation, oral or written, will vary widely according to the occasion and our individual needs. In academic and workplace settings, we read so that we can make informed contributions to a conversation that is already in progress. Indeed, we are expected to join in.

Entering an oral conversation can sometimes be a simple process of responding to a question. ("Have you seen the new film at the Ridgemont?") But if a conversation is already well under way, finding an opening can sometimes be a complex process of getting people's attention and staking claim to authority on a subject. ("Um, you know, I've seen all of John Woo's films, and I think. . . .") The challenge is even greater if the goal is to redirect the conversation or contradict the prevailing opinion. ("Yes, but listen! The reading I've done for my cinematography class tells me that his action films are not as innovative as the ads claim.") When we take up writing as a way of entering the conversation, we don't have to worry about interrupting, but we do have to review the conversation for our readers by laying out introductory background.

To explore the similarities between your motives for joining a conversation and your motives for reading, consider how the influential twentieth-century rhetorician and philosopher Kenneth Burke uses conversation as a metaphor for reading and writing:

> Imagine you enter a parlor. You come late. When you arrive, others have long preceded you, and they are engaged in a heated discussion, a discussion too heated for them to pause and tell you exactly what it is about. In fact, the discussion had already begun long before any of them got there, so that no one present is qualified to retrace for you all the steps that had gone before. You

listen for a while, until you decide that you have caught the tenor of the argument; then you put in your oar. Someone answers; you answer him; another comes to your defense; another aligns himself against you, to either the embarrassment or gratification of your opponent, depending upon the quality of your ally's assistance. However, the discussion is interminable. The hour grows late, you must depart. And you do depart, with the discussion still vigorously in progress.[1]

FOR WRITING AND DISCUSSION

To explore the implications of Burke's parlor metaphor for your own reading processes, consider the following questions.

ON YOUR OWN

1. In what ways does Burke's parlor metaphor fit your experience? Freewrite for a few minutes about an oral conversation in which you managed to assert your voice—or "put in your oar," as Burke says—after listening for a while, or about a situation where reading helped you gather a sense of the general flow of ideas so that you could have something to say about a topic.
2. Consider a community that you belong to where you feel that you can quickly catch the drift of an in-progress conversation (e.g., other triathlon athletes, or regulars on *Farmville*). What are some "hot topics" of conversation in these communities? What might exclude someone from these conversations? If you wanted to address a general audience about this issue, how much background information would you need to supply?
3. Now let's reverse the situation. Have you ever listened to a conversation in which you were a baffled outsider rather than an insider? Describe an experience where you had to work hard to get inside an ongoing conversation. Then consider how that experience might be an appropriate analogy for a time when you were frustrated by trying to read a book or article addressed to an insider audience rather than to someone with your background.

WITH YOUR CLASSMATES

Share your responses with other members of your class. See if others have had experiences similar to yours. What have been the topics of conversations where they were in "insider" and "outsider" roles? Help each other appreciate the concepts of insider and outsider audiences and of reading as joining a conversation.

---

[1]Kenneth Burke, *The Philosophy of Literary Form: Studies in Symbolic Action*, 3rd ed. (Berkeley: U of California P, 1973), 110–11. Print.

Reading and Writing as Acts of Composing

The give and take of oral conversation connects naturally to our second meta-phor, reading as an act of composing. The idea that writing is an act of compos-ing is probably familiar to you. Indeed, the terms *writing* and *composing* are often used interchangeably. Originally associated with fine arts such as paint-ing, music, or literary writing, the term *composing* still carries with it the idea of originality or creativity, even though it has come to mean the production of any kind of written text, from a memo to a prize-winning novel. Unlike the term *writing*, the word *composing* suggests more than the mere transcription of a preexisting meaning or idea. Instead, it suggests a creative putting together of words and ideas to make a new whole. Except for the act of literally recopying what someone else has written, all writing, even memo writing, is a matter of selecting and arranging language to accomplish a purpose that is unique to a particular situation and audience.

However, the idea that reading is an act of composing may be less familiar. The ancients thought of reading as a passive activity in which the author, via the text, deposited meaning in a reader—the text was metaphorically (or even literally) "consumed." The Old Testament prophet Ezekiel, for example, has a vision in which he is instructed by the Lord to open his mouth and literally consume a book that gives him the knowledge he needs to speak to the rebel-lious Israelites. Commenting on the consumption metaphors associated with reading, Alberto Manguel, in *A History of Reading*, notes the parallels between the cooking metaphors associated with writing—the author "cooks up" a plot or "spices" up her introduction—and the eating metaphors associated with reading—the reader "devours" a book, finds "nourishment" in it, then "regur-gitates" what he has read.[2] Although the image of Ezekiel's eating of a text seems fantastic, the mistaken idea persists that reading is a one-way transac-tion: author → text → reader. To illustrate the flaws in this model of the reading process, let's try a simple experiment described by reading researcher Kathleen McCormick. Read the following passage and jot down your interpretation of its meaning:

> Tony slowly got up from the mat, planning his escape. He hesitated a moment and thought. Things were not going well. What bothered him most was being held, especially since the charge against him had been weak. He considered his present situation. The lock that held him was strong but he thought he could break it. . . . He was being ridden unmercifully. . . . He felt that he was ready to make his move.[3]

There are two common interpretations: readers assume that Tony is either in jail or in a wrestling match. Unless you are familiar with wrestling, you likely

---

[2]Alberto Manguel, *A History of Reading* (New York: Penguin, 1997), 170–71. Print.
[3]Kathleen McCormick, *The Culture of Reading and the Teaching of English* (Manchester, England: Manchester UP, 1994), 20–21. Print.

thought Tony was a prisoner planning a jailbreak. However, if this paragraph appeared in a short story about a wrestler, you would immediately assume that "mat," "escape," "charge," "being held," and "lock" referred to wrestling even if you knew very little about the sport. This experiment demonstrates two important aspects of the reading process: (1) readers use their previous experiences and knowledge to create meaning from what they read; and (2) context influences meaning.

Research such as McCormick's shows that readers make sense of a text not by passively receiving meaning from it, but by actively composing a reading of it. This composing process links the reader's existing knowledge and ideas with the new information in the text. What the reader brings to the text is as important as the text itself. In other words, reading is not a process in which an author simply transfers information to the reader. Rather, it is a dynamic process in which the reader's worldview interacts with the writer's worldview. The reader constructs meaning from the text, in effect creating a new "text" in the reader's mind. The new text is the reader's active interpretation of the text being read.

When college writing assignments ask you to explain and support your reading (or interpretation) of a text, whether verbal or visual, it is important to distinguish between *private* associations that are only loosely related to the text and interpretations that are *publicly* defensible in terms of textual evidence. Private associations are one-way responses in which a certain word, image, or idea in a text sends you off into your own world, causing you to lose track of the network of cues in the text as a whole. Although such private responses are natural, and indeed one of the pleasures of reading, if you are to offer a public interpretation, you must engage in a two-way interaction with a text, attending to both its network of cues and your personal responses and associations with it. In short, "good" or sound interpretations are those that are supported by textual evidence and thus are understandable as well as persuasive to other readers, whose experiences and beliefs are probably different from yours.

Reading Rhetorically as a Strategy for Academic Writing

The metaphors of conversation and composing bring out the essential rhetorical nature of reading and writing. By **rhetorical,** we mean "related to an intended effect." Invoking the term "rhetoric" always draws attention to a writer's relationship to and intentions toward an audience. Consider Aristotle's definition of rhetoric as the art of discovering the available means of persuasion in a given situation. Although the word "persuasion" focuses on an audience, Aristotle's definition highlights **discovery** along with **persuasion.** From this pairing, we can understand that writers must thoroughly understand their subject in order to discover the best methods for presenting their material to others. By "best," we mean the most ethically responsible as well as the most persuasive. Rhetoric's partnership of discovery and persuasion makes it clear why reading

...ically is a powerful academic strategy in all disciplines. When you read rhetorically, you read with awareness of both the purposes of the author whose text you are reading and your own purposes as a reader and writer.

The Purposes of the Author Whose Text You Are Reading

When we introduced the term *reading rhetorically* early in this chapter, we described authors as having designs on their readers. That phrasing underscores the fact that writers want to change readers' perceptions and thinking, and that they use both direct and indirect means to do so. Typically, a writer's goal is to change a reader's understanding of subject matter in some way. Sometimes the change might simply confirm what the reader thought beforehand—readers typically enjoy music and film reviews that affirm their own opinions and political columns that echo their views. At other times, the change might involve an increase in knowledge or in clarity of understanding (an article explaining how bluenose dolphins use whistling sounds to converse with each other might increase your awe of sea mammals). Sometimes the change might radically reconstruct a reader's whole view of a subject (an article reporting new scientific evidence might convince you to reverse your position on legalization of medical marijuana). How much change occurs as a result of reading? The reader decides.

Your Own Purposes as an Active Reader/Writer

When an assignment asks you to respond in some way to texts that you have read, you must take on the role of an active reader who composes meanings. Your responses might range from writing marginal notes on the text itself (something that expert readers do) to posting an entry on your class online discussion forum to writing a major research paper. Your decisions about the way you will read a text and think critically about it will depend upon your own purposes as a writer.

Questions Rhetorical Readers Ask

You can begin the practice of reading rhetorically by asking the eight analytical questions that follow when you encounter new texts. Whether you are reading the abstract of a scientific article or comments posted on a forum about R&B styling, these questions will help you discover how a writer's purpose and worldview become evident in a text. These insights, in turn, will help you analyze how a given text works so that you can decide how you want to respond to it and use it in your own writing.

1. What questions does the text address, explicitly or implicitly? (Why are these significant questions? What community cares about them?)

2. Who is the intended audience? (Am I part of this audience or an outsider?)
3. How does the author support his or her thesis with reasons and evidence? (Do I find this argument convincing? What views and counterarguments are omitted from the text? What counterevidence is ignored?)
4. How does the author hook the intended reader's interest and keep the reader reading? (Do these appeals work for me? Do they make me suspicious of the author's motives?)
5. How does the author make himself or herself seem credible to the intended audience? (Is the author credible for me? Are the author's sources reliable?)
6. Are this writer's basic values, beliefs, and assumptions similar to or different from my own? (How does this writer's worldview accord with mine?)
7. How do I respond to this text? (Will I go along with or challenge what this text is presenting? How has it changed my thinking?)
8. How do this author's evident purposes for writing fit with my purposes for reading? (How will I be able to use what I have learned from the text?)

● FOR WRITING AND DISCUSSION

The Questions Rhetorical Readers Ask are useful for analyzing visual as well as verbal texts. To demonstrate the power of rhetorical reading, we invite you to use the questions above to analyze how the image in Figure 1.1 attempts to influence the thinking of viewers/readers. How effective is it? (In Chapters 3 and 4, we offer some specific advice on how to do a rhetorical analysis of visual texts such as this one.)

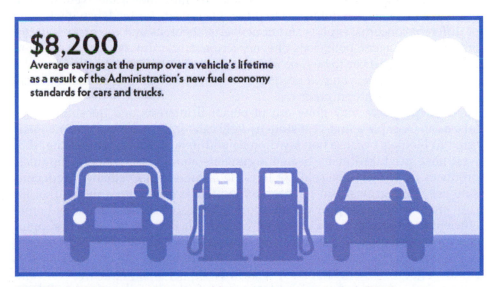

FIGURE 1.1 Whitehouse.gov Web page praising new fuel economy standards (2012)

Working alone or with classmates, use the eight questions to consider how the verbal and visual elements work to engage you and make a point. Are the words or the images more important? We suspect you will say "words," which leads to this question: Why are the images there at all? Of course, without having the designers available to ask, you can't know the answer for certain. However, just by considering the information in the caption you can start to build a context for the visual text. Then you can evaluate how well this combination of text and pictures works to accomplish what you take to be its purpose.

Our purpose here is to demonstrate that by exploring your own responses to the images and text (and hearing about others' responses), you can gain some insight into the ways that words and images work together to engage readers—that is, how they work rhetorically. In Chapters 3 and 4, we will offer more specific advice about how to do rhetorical analysis of visual texts such as this one, including categories of purpose.   •

An Extended Example: Researching the Promise of Biofuels

Imagine that your instructor in a geography or political science class assigns a major research paper that will require you to find and select your own sources. These potential sources (there may be hundreds of possibilities) will pose reading challenges different from those of your course textbooks because these sources will be written for many different audiences and purposes by authors with varied credentials on the subject. On any given topic—let's take the development of biofuels as a broad example—it's likely your research will turn up scholarly articles, popular magazine articles, news reports, a few books, and a range of politically charged editorials, op-ed columns, blogs, and Web sites. All of them will have been published in different contexts for readers with a range of different concerns: experts and nonexperts, theorists and researchers, farmers and automakers, politicians of every stripe, and ordinary citizens trying to figure out the best car to buy, or which politician to vote for. As a reader who is planning to write, you will need to determine what, among all this material, suits *your* needs and purposes.

Your purposes may grow out of personal interests and questions. Let's take as an example a first-year student we'll call "Jack," who has become interested in biofuels because holiday dinners with relatives who farm in the Midwest have produced many heated arguments about corn ethanol. One uncle produces feed corn to be sold not to cattle farmers, but to ethanol producers. Another uncle grows corn for people food. He is certain that the market for corn ethanol will disappear within a couple of years because cleaner and more efficiently produced biofuels will be developed. Both of these men support environmental causes, and each feels that his choice about what kind of corn to grow will be better for the environment. Additionally, one uncle argues that producing corn ethanol contributes to U.S. energy independence; the other argues that using good farmland to produce fuel rather than food will have negative consequences. These dinner-table conversations became even more intense after Congress ended federal tax breaks for companies that produce gasoline mixed with ethanol.

Motivated by curiosity about which of his uncles might be making the better choice, Jack decides to write a paper for his political science class about the pros and cons of growing corn for ethanol production. During class discussion, he gains and shares insights with a classmate who grew up in a big city and is writing about corn ethanol from the perspective of consumers who are environmentalists, asking whether it really is a clean fuel. They are both aware of intense debates around these issues, as reflected in the visual arguments represented in Figures 1.2 and 1.3, and they agree that their goals are to gather information for their papers, not controversial arguments.

Despite a wealth of readily available materials on the subject, both students eventually find themselves hard pressed to provide definite answers to their questions. Searches of periodicals databases uncover a wealth of materials on ethanol and other biofuels, but the conclusions seem almost contradictory. Published reports indicate that despite the end of federal tax subsidies for ethanol producers, the amount of corn grown for ethanol continues to increase. Meanwhile, university professors and oil companies receive press coverage for their research about the practicality of using other biofuels to run gasoline engines.

Web searches turn up a wide range of perspectives on ethanol, from industry groups supporting expanded corn ethanol production, to oil companies boasting of their commitment to alternative fuels, to environmental organizations opposing the use of farmland for biofuel development. Furthermore,

FIGURE 1.2 Illinois billboard advertising corn seed hybridized for ethanol production from Pioneer Hi-Bred International, Inc.

FIGURE 1.3 Editorial cartoon by Robert Ariail

Jack's classmate discovers that environmental groups have been arguing not only that the fuel is not particularly clean or efficient but also that ethanol production is actually bad for the environment. Between them, they discover that, as yet, there is no clear answer about the wisdom of developing corn ethanol for automotive fuel, nor about the trade-offs of using agricultural land for developing biofuels.

In other words, Jack and his friend learn that there is not one "ethanol debate." There are many, depending on the interests and values of the debaters. Jack discovers that he must recognize and investigate the perspectives not only of farmers like his uncles, but also of environmental organizations, producers of ethanol and gasoline, investors in alternative fuels, scientists (who want hard evidence), government agencies (who rely on the scientists' research), manufacturers of gasoline engines—and ordinary consumers shopping for a car that fits their values and pocketbook. (Excerpts from Jack's research log are in Chapter 5. His paper about multiple perspectives on biofuels appears at the end of Chapter 6.)

Jack's experience illustrates our larger point that only careful reading will lead to a good academic paper on a complex subject. Reading rhetorically is a powerful academic skill that will help you recognize the persuasive strategies built into many different kinds of texts. Inevitably, no text tells the whole story. A reader needs to focus not only on what a given text says but on its rhetorical strategies for making its case. To promote an argument, some texts will distort opposing perspectives; others will make certain perspectives invisible. A headline on the Web about "Biofuels' Potential to Revolutionize the Global Economy" may primarily be a pitch to interest investors in a start-up company. The organization behind a headline announcing an article about the "Pros and Cons of Ethanol" might be a trade association that lobbies for (or against) corn ethanol, or it could be a lone environmental blogger repackaging reports of unknown reliability. Eventually, after you (like Jack) have read enough materials from sources you have learned to trust, by writers you learn to respect (in part by checking their credentials), you will be able to fill in background that you perhaps did not even notice was missing when you first started reading in a given subject area.

How can you tell whether a text seeks to give you a full picture in a fair and reliable manner or is simply making another one-sided argument about a hotly contested issue? By learning to read rhetorically. Doing so will enable you to read—and then write—successful college papers.

Chapter Summary

In this chapter, we have defined the concept of reading rhetorically, and explained how practicing it can help you be successful with a wide variety of college writing assignments. In the preceding pages, we

- Defined rhetorical reading as paying attention to both the content of a text ("what") and the author's method of presenting that content ("how")
- Described the special demands and pleasures of academic reading, which often requires recognizing how different academic disciplines value evidence and report research
- Used the metaphors of conversation and composing to describe how both reading and writing are active processes through which readers construe a text's meaning by bringing their own values and experiences to it and articulating their own ideas in response
- Provided a list of eight questions rhetorical readers use to judge how a text works and how to respond to it
- Showed the value of rhetorical reading as an academic strategy through which a reader analyzes a text's content and strategies in order to decide how to respond—whether to assent to the writer's ideas, modify them, or resist them

In the chapters that follow, we will offer you a variety of strategies that are likely to bring you success as you respond to assignments like these by using rhetorical reading skills to work with the texts upon which your writing will be based.

CHAPTER 2

Analyzing Your Reading and Writing Context

*It is like the rubbing of two sticks together to make a fire,
the act of reading, an improbable pedestrian task that leads to
heat and light.*

—Anna Quindlen

Here is this chapter's point in a nutshell: Writers write for a purpose to an audience within a genre. Together, these three factors—purpose, audience, and genre—create what we call "**rhetorical context**." The more aware you are of these factors, the more efficient you will be as a reader and the more effective you will be as a writer. Analyzing a text's rhetorical context as you read will enable you to frame a response in terms of your own rhetorical context: What will be your purpose, audience, and genre? Your answers will influence not only what you write but also the way you read and use additional texts.

In this chapter, you will learn

- To analyze a text's original rhetorical context (purpose, audience, and genre)
- To analyze your own rhetorical context for reading
- To adapt experts' reading strategies and make your reading more efficient
    - By using genre knowledge
    - By analyzing the text's original social/historical context
- To recognize the major role reading plays in different types of college writing assignments

Rhetorical Context: Purpose, Audience, and Genre

Recognizing the influence of rhetorical context helps rhetorical readers reconstruct the strategy behind an author's choices about content (for example, what to include and exclude), structure (for example, what to say first, when to reveal the thesis, how to arrange the parts, how to format the document), and style (whether to use big words or ordinary words, complex or easy sentence structure, lots of jargon or no jargon, and so forth).

Analyzing an Author's Purpose

In Chapter 1 we noted that writers have designs on readers—that is, writers aim to change a reader's view of a subject in some way. They might aim to enlarge a reader's view of a subject, clarify that view, or restructure that view. This motive to reach out to an audience through language inevitably stems from some problem or perceived misunderstanding or gap in knowledge that an author wishes to remedy. Rhetorician Lloyd F. Bitzer used the term **exigence** for a flaw that an author believes can be altered by a text presented to an audience.[1] This flaw might be a circumstance that is other than it should be, a situation in need of attention, or perhaps an occasion in need of special recognition. Your ability as a reader to pinpoint an author's sense of a flaw, a problem, or some other situation in need of change will enable you to zero in on that author's purpose. Furthermore, when you are ready to write about what you have read, thinking of your purpose as writing in order to remedy a flaw will help you focus sharply. Such "flaws" or problems may be as simple as the need to provide information or as complex as the need to advocate for standardizing a set of medical procedures in order to reduce infections. (You will see surgeon Atul Gawande make this argument in the reading at the end of Chapter 4.) For example, you might need to inform a potential employer of your availability and qualifications for a particular job, so you submit a letter and résumé. Or you could need to demonstrate to a history professor that you do, indeed, have a good grasp of the economic system that dominated during China's Ming dynasty, so you answer an exam question with careful detail.

A set of categories for conceptualizing the ways that writers aim to change readers' minds is summarized in Table 2.1 (see pp. 19–20). Based on a scheme developed by rhetoricians to categorize types of discourse in terms of a writer's aim or purpose, the table identifies eight **rhetorical aims** or purposes that writers typically set for themselves. This framework offers a particularly powerful way of thinking about both reading and writing because each row zeroes in on

---

[1]Bitzer's concept of an exigence within a *rhetorical situation*, modified over the years, was first described in his essay, "The Rhetorical Situation," *Philosophy and Rhetoric* 1.1 (1968): 1–14. *EbscoHost.* Web. 3 June 2012.

TABLE 2.1 ● A SPECTRUM OF PURPOSES

Rhetorical Aim	Focus and Features	Desired Response	Examples
Express and Reflect **Offers Readers:** Shared emotional, intellectual experience	**Focus:** Writer's own life and experience **Features:** Literary techniques such as plot, character, setting, evocative language	**Readers** can imagine and identify with writer's experience. **Success** depends on writer's ability to create scenes, dialog, and commentary that engage readers.	Nursing student reflects on her semester of Service Learning at a school for young children with developmental delays and disabilities.
Inquire and Explore **Offers Readers:** Shared intellectual experience, new information, new perspectives	**Focus:** Puzzling problem seen through narration of writer's thinking processes **Features:** Delayed thesis or no thesis; examination of subject from multiple angles; writer's thinking is foregrounded.	**Readers** will agree question or problem is significant, identify with writer's thinking, and find new insights. **Success** depends on writer's ability to engage readers with question or problem and the exploration process.	Students in an honors seminar taught by a physicist and philosopher write papers that explore the question: "What makes study of the origins of the universe significant to daily life in the twenty-first century?"
Inform and Explain **(also called *expository writing*)** **Offers Readers:** Significant, perhaps surprising, new information; presentation tailored to readers' interest and presumed knowledge level	**Focus:** Subject matter **Features:** Confident, authoritative stance; typically states point and purpose early; strives for clarity; provides definitions and examples; uses convincing evidence without argument	**Readers** will grant writer credibility as expert, and be satisfied with the information's scope and accuracy. **Success** depends on writer's ability to anticipate readers' information needs and ability to understand.	Economics intern is assigned to track 10 years of the rise and fall of mortgage interest rates and report on experts' current explanations of the trends.
Analyze and Interpret **Offers Readers:** New way of looking at the subject matter	**Focus:** Phenomena that are difficult to understand or explain **Features:** Relatively tentative stance; thesis supported by evidence and reasoning; new or unsettling analyses and interpretations must be convincing; doesn't assume that evidence speaks for itself	**Readers** will grant writer credibility as analyst and accept insights offered, or at least acknowledge value of approach. **Success** depends on writer's ability to explain reasoning and connect it with phenomena analyzed.	Literature student analyzes the definition of *justice* employed by various characters in Sophocles' play *Antigone* with the goal of interpreting the author's understanding of the concept.

(continued)

TABLE 2.1 • A SPECTRUM OF PURPOSES (CONTINUED)

Rhetorical Aim	Focus and Features	Desired Response	Examples
Persuasion: **Take a Stand** **Offers Readers:** Reasons to make up or change their minds about a question at issue	**Focus:** Question that divides a community **Features:** States a firm position, provides clear reasons and evidence, connects with readers' values and beliefs, engages with opposing views	**Readers** will agree with writer's position and reasoning. **Success** depends on writer's ability to provide convincing support and to counter opposition without alienating readers.	For an ethics class, an architecture student decides to write an argument in favor of placing certain buildings in his community on the historic preservation register, thus preserving them from demolition or radical remodeling.
Persuasion: **Evaluate and Judge** **Offers Readers:** Reasons to make up or change their minds about a focal question regarding worth or value	**Focus:** Question about worth or value of a phenomenon **Features:** Organized around criteria for judgment and how phenomenon matches them	**Readers** will accept writer's view of the worth or value of the phenomenon. **Success** depends on writer's ability to connect subject to criteria that readers accept.	Political theory students are asked to evaluate and choose between the descriptions of an ideal ruler embodied in Plato's philosopher king and Machiavelli's prince.
Persuasion: **Propose a Solution** **Offers Readers:** A recommended course of action	**Focus:** Question about what action should be taken **Features:** Describes problem and solution, then justifies solution in terms of values and consequences; level of detail depends on assumptions about readers' knowledge	**Readers** will assent to proposed action and do as writer suggests. **Success** depends on readers' agreement that a problem exists and/or that the recommended action will have good results.	A group of seniors majoring in social welfare collaborates on a grant proposal to a community foundation interested in improving health education in a rural area.
Persuasion: **Seek Common Ground** **Offers Readers:** New perspectives and reduced intensity regarding difficult issues	**Focus:** Multiple perspectives on a vexing problem **Features:** Lays out the values and goals of the various stakeholders so that others can find commonalities to build on; does not advocate	**Readers** will discover mutuality with opponents; conflict may not be resolved; discussion could lead to cooperative action. **Success** depends on readers' discovery of mutual interests.	An environmental studies student designs a thesis project to interview advocates and stakeholders who are divided over a proposal to remove a dam from a major river; her goal is to find and highlight points of agreement.

how a writer might envision a purpose that connects subject matter to audience in a given rhetorical situation. In the table, we describe how texts in each category work, what they offer readers, and the response their authors typically aim to bring about. The table illustrates the differences among the aims with examples of texts that a college student might compose in response to assignments in a variety of courses.

We have labeled the table's third column "Desired Response" because we want to emphasize that a writer can only *desire* a certain response from a reader; they cannot assume or force that response. The reader is in charge because it is the reader who decides whether to accede to the writer's intentions or to resist them. Because writers try to persuade an intended audience to adopt their perspective, they select and arrange evidence, choose examples, include or omit material, and select words and images to best support their perspective. But readers are the ones who decide—sometimes unconsciously, sometimes deliberately—whether the presentation is convincing. Your awareness of how a text is constructed to persuade its intended audience will enable you to decide how you want to respond to that text and use it in your own writing.

● FOR WRITING AND DISCUSSION

To explore the spectrum of aims presented in Table 2.1, choose an issue or situation that interests you and fill in the grid of a similar table with sample writing scenarios and purposes for each of the table's eight rows of rhetorical aims. Working alone or with others, fill in as many cells in the example column as you can. Choose from the following hypothetical writers or another writer-reader combination that intrigues you in connection with the topic you choose.

- College students in a variety of courses
- A single writer (perhaps an entertainment columnist or a sports writer) seeking publication in a variety of venues, including the Web, about the same subject matter
- People in a variety of roles writing with different aims about the same topic (perhaps a family matter such as pets or divorce, or a public matter such as green energy or human rights) ●

Identifying an Author's Intended Audience

Audience plays a major role in guiding an author's choices. As you analyze a text, watch for cues in the author's language and use of detail that reveal assumptions about the intended audience.

For example, suppose a writer wants to persuade legislators to raise gasoline taxes in order to reduce fossil fuel consumption. Her strategy might be to persuade different groups of voters to pressure their congressional representatives. If she writes for a scientific audience, her article can include technical data and detailed statistical analyses. If she addresses the general public, however,

ANALYZING AN AUTHOR'S DESIGNS ON YOUR THINKING

One way to analyze an author's purpose is to consider the kind of change the author hopes to bring about in readers' minds. Try using this formula to quiz yourself about the author's desire to change your mind:

At the beginning of the text, the writer assumes that the reader believes
_____.

By the end of the text, the writer hopes that the reader believes _____
_____.

These questions will help you, as a rhetorical reader, to analyze your own response to the text—whether you are going to think or do what the writer apparently hopes you will.

her style will have to be less technical and more lively, with storylike anecdotes rather than tabular data. If she writes for an environmental publication, she can assume an audience already supportive of her pro-environment values. However, if she writes for a business publication such as the *Wall Street Journal*, she will have to be sensitive to her audience's pro-business values—perhaps by arguing that what is good for the environment will be good for business in the long run.

Analyzing a Text's Genre

As writers respond to rhetorical situations by adapting content, structure, and style to different purposes and audiences, they must also adapt to the conventions of a text's **genre**, a term that refers to a recurring category or type of writing based on identifiable features such as structure (for example, a thesis-driven argument or an informal reflection) and document design (for example, the format of academic papers, Web pages, or promotional brochures). These genre-based decisions about format include whether to add visual images, and, if so, what kind will be appropriate and effective. Because particular textual features are expected in particular situations, a writer's effort to follow or modify genre conventions can become a valuable tool for engaging readers and moving them toward desired responses such as those indicated in Table 2.1.

You may be familiar with the concept of genre from literature classes where you studied an assortment of genres, such as plays, novels, and poems. Within each of these broad literary genres are subgenres such as the sonnet and haiku or tragedy and comedy. Similarly, workplace writing has a number of subgenres (memos, marketing proposals, financial reports, progress reports) as

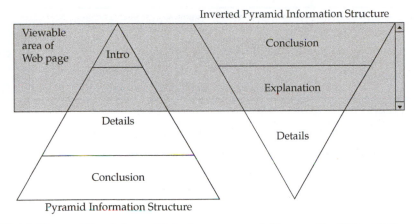

FIGURE 2.1 Diagram of inverted pyramid structure recommended for organizing Web content

does academic writing (laboratory reports, field notes, article abstracts, literature reviews). As the descriptions of typical college writing assignments later in
this chapter show, even familiar academic assignments have subgenres (informal response papers, essay exams, article summaries, or researched arguments
that present a semester's worth of work).

Consider one commonly encountered genre: the **inverted pyramid** of a
news article, in print or online. These reports begin with the key facts of a news
event—*who, what, when, where, why*, and *how*—before offering background information and details. As Figure 2.1 shows, a similar structure is recommended
for Web writing, where it is necessary to capture readers' attention quickly, in
the limited amount of space immediately visible on a screen.

In both cases, someone in a hurry or with only a passing interest in the
subject matter should be able to glean the gist of the news or of the Web site's
purpose by reading just the initial sentences. Furthermore, on Web sites, putting the essential facts first makes it easier for search engines to spot and report
on the page's content.

Genre differences in written texts frequently become evident through visual cues, and these cues in turn create reader expectations. The Web site of
the *New York Times* uses typefaces and layout that resemble those of its paper
edition, but the home page of a veterinary clinic (interested in inviting new
patients) will likely be different from the home page of an advice blog about
caring for exotic birds. Similarly, genre differences influence the look of print
documents. If you were browsing publications in the current periodicals rack
at a library, you could quickly distinguish popular magazines such as *Popular
Science* and *Business Week* from scholarly journals such as the *American Journal
of Human Genetics* or the *Journal of Marketing Research*. The glossy covers of the
magazines, often adorned with arresting photographs, distinguish them from
sober-looking scholarly journals, the covers of which typically display a table of
contents of the articles within. (These genre distinctions are less apparent when

FIGURE 2.2 Image from page 1 of a research report the scholarly journal *Appetite* about the fleeting cognitive benefits of gum-chewing

you are browsing through articles in a computerized periodicals database, a challenge we address in Chapter 5.) As you develop your ability to recognize genres and the ways that their conventions shape content, you will also sharpen your ability to decide whether and how to use particular texts for your own purposes.

As illustration, consider the distinctive differences between the genres of the two articles introduced by the images in Figures 2.2 and 2.3. As the captions indicate, the first is taken from the scholarly journal *Appetite* and the second was originally published in a monthly health newsletter, the *UC Berkeley Wellness Letter*. A quick glance makes evident the differences in these texts' rhetorical contexts, from the different page layouts to the contrasts between casual language and formal vocabulary.

The article from *Appetite* depicted in Figure 2.2 is one of two studies from the October 2011 issue that were used by a staff writer for the *Wellness Letter* to produce "Chew on This"—a short, easy-to-read summary of recent research on gum-chewing (presented in full in Figure 2.3). This piece was written to catch

Chew on This ← ——————— Punning Title

Most people chew gum for pleasure or out of habit; others to freshen breath or stop a food or cigarette craving. Does gum provide any real benefits? There have been lots of studies on gum over the years, including two recent ones.

The best evidence concerns gum's ability to prevent cavities by boosting saliva flow and neutralizing acid produced by mouth bacteria. Sugar-free gums are best for this, notably those with the sugar alcohol xylitol, which suppresses the growth of cavity-producing bacteria. Still, gum can't replace brushing and flossing.

Can gum make you thinner? Gum chewing burns only about 11 calories an hour. But if it keeps you from eating a candy bar, that's a big plus. Studies on whether gum reduces appetite have produced conflicting findings. The latest study, in the journal *Appetite* found that when women chewed gum (15 minutes, once an hour, for three hours), they ate about 30 fewer calories when subsequently offered a snack compared to when they hadn't chewed gum. The women also said they felt less hungry and fuller after chewing the gum. Gum manufacturers have helped publicize these results. But each piece of gum had 5 to 10 calories, so the women didn't actually cut down on calories significantly. Would sugarless gum have had the same effect? Maybe, maybe not.

Informal language in attention-getting questions

Closes with scholarly quote followed by joking paraphrase.

Make you smarter? Some early research found that gum chewing improved performance on memory tests, perhaps by boosting blood flow to the brain and stimulating a part of the brain where information is processed. But more recent studies have failed to find any brain benefit—or have noted that gum sometimes worsens performance.

Another recent study in *Appetite* found that gum improved performance on certain cognitive tests, but only when it was chewed before, not during, the tests. The benefit lasted just 15 to 20 minutes. According to the researchers, gum doesn't help thinking—and possibly even impairs it—during a task because of "interference due to a sharing of metabolic resources by cognitive and masticatory processes." In other words, some people can't think (or walk) and chew gum at the same time.

FIGURE 2.3 Text of the "Last Word" column on the last page (p. 8) of the *UC Berkeley Wellness Letter*, Feb. 2012. Note that the journal that published the original research, *Appetite,* is mentioned only briefly (as highlighted in the figure).

the attention of casual readers whose curiosity might be piqued by the clever title and the questions about the effects of chewing gum placed in bold-face headings, questions that readers will discover do not have definitive answers. Contrast this informal article with the formality and detail evident on the first page of the *Appetite* article in Figure 2.2. Despite the playful wording in the title—"Cognitive Advantages of Chewing Gum. Now You See them, Now You Don't"—the overall presentation of the opening page signals that it is a scholarly research report, including the label at the upper left labeling it as such. Scholarly elements highlighted by the labels and circles in the figure include the names of four authors (with an asterisk indicating the one to whom correspondence may be sent), a history of the article's submission to the journal, an abstract, a keywords list, and an introduction reviewing the literature from previous studies on the topic. The article's remaining seven pages describe in detail the methodology of two studies about gum-chewing and test-taking behaviors, present charts and graphs of the results, and discuss the significance of those results.

Casual readers are likely to respond positively to the newsletter's brief summary of the research, but the readers of the scholarly journal are looking for more than lighthearted advice about gum-chewing. The *Appetite* article's intended audience is other researchers, not the general public. The keywords list will help those researchers find this article so that they can read about both its findings and methodology. As is customary, the article's last page suggests what work needs to be done by subsequent researchers: "In summary, the current study demonstrates that the discrepancies in research findings of the burgeoning literature on the effect of gum chewing on cognitive function can be attributed to the timing of chewing....further studies are needed to provide a more complete picture of the relationship between physiological changes and cognitive functioning due to the chewing of gum." (Onyper et al., 327—see full citation below).[2]

From dense scientific research reports like this, the unnamed author of "Chew on This" used expert reading skills to dig out key points of information—and ambiguity—and transform them into a lively little article designed to spark a few smiles as well.[3] This reader-writer might have been trained as a journalist, or might be a graduate student in psychology or public health who will go on to build a career by publishing in journals like *Appetite*. In the pages ahead, we suggest strategies for you as both reader and writer for developing your own abilities to work with and for a variety of audiences, purposes, and genres.

● **FOR WRITING AND DISCUSSION**

Both of the scholarly articles about gum-chewing from the October 2011 issue of *Appetite* (see full citations in footnotes 2 and 3) should be available through your school library, probably electronically. We invite you to explore in more detail the genre differences between them and the newsletter article in Figure 2.3. If your library also subscribes to the *UC Berkeley Wellness Letter,* you will have an opportunity to note contrasting genre features in that publication as well. ●

---

[2]Serge V. Onyper, et al., "Cognitive Advantages of Chewing Gum. Now You See Them, Now You Don't." *Appetite* 57.2 (2011): 321–328. *Science Direct*. Web. 9 June 2012.

[3]The *Appetite* article about gum-chewing and snacking is by Marion M. Hetherington and Martin F. Regan, "Effects of Chewing Gum on Short-Term Appetite Regulation in Moderately Restrained Eaters." *Appetite* 57.2 (2011): 475–482. *Science Direct*. Web. 9 June 2012.

Analyzing Your Own Rhetorical Context as Reader/Writer

When you are assigned to read texts of any type (a textbook, a scholarly article, data on a Web site, historical documents, or other kinds of readings), think not only about the authors' rhetorical context, but also about your own.

Determining Your Purpose, Audience, and Genre

When you write about various texts or use them in your own arguments, you will be writing for a purpose to an audience within a genre. In college, your purpose will be determined by your assignment. (See the final section of this chapter, "Typical Reading-Based Writing Assignments Across the Curriculum," pp. 32–37.) Your audience may range from yourself to your professor and your classmates, to readers of a certain newspaper or blog, even to participants in an undergraduate research conference. Your assigned genre might come from a wide range of possibilities: summary, Web posting, rhetorical analysis, reader-response reflection, source-based argument, or a major research paper.

Identifying your purpose at the outset helps you set goals and plan your reading accordingly. Your purpose for reading may seem like a self-evident matter—"I'm reading Chapter 1 of this sociology book because it was assigned for tomorrow." That may be, but what we have in mind is a more strategic consideration of your purpose. Ask yourself how the reading assignment ties in with themes established in class. How does it fit with concepts laid out on the course syllabus? Is this your first course in sociology? If so, you might set a purpose for yourself of gathering definitions of the foundational concepts and specialized vocabulary used by sociologists. These basic but strategically stated goals might lead you to allow extra time for the slowed-down reading that students usually need in order to get their bearings at the beginning of introductory courses.

To illustrate the importance of establishing purposes for your reading, let's move farther into the semester and assume you are skimming articles to select some for closer reading and possible use in an annotated bibliography for this first course in sociology. Further, imagine that your assignment is to choose and summarize articles that demonstrate how sociological research can shed light on a current public controversy. As we discuss in detail in Chapter 5, an important first step in an assignment like this is to identify a clear and compelling **research question**. A strong research question will enable you to know what you're looking for, and it will guide you to read more purposefully and productively. Let's say you are interested in whether pop culture has a negative effect on family values. You want to think that it doesn't, but from sometimes intense discussions among family and friends, you realize that the answer might be "it depends." Maybe sociological research has laid out some systematic ways of thinking about this issue, and a more productive question would be "How does pop culture impact family values?" or "What is known about how pop culture impacts family values?"

Following the demands of your research question, you will need to define both "pop culture" and "family values" and narrow your focus as you find articles related to your controversy. Some sources will report research findings contrary to your own views; others will tend to confirm your views. To summarize them fairly, you will have to pay careful attention to the way these authors articulate their own research questions and present their results. Setting goals ahead of time for both your writing and your reading will help you know what to look for as you select and read articles.

Matching Your Reading Strategies to Your Purpose as Reader/Writer

Although all readers change their approach to reading according to their audience, purpose, and the genre of the text at hand, most readers do so without thought or reflection, relying on a limited set of strategies. By contrast, experienced readers vary their reading process self-consciously and strategically. To see how one accomplished undergraduate, Sheri, contrasts her "school" reading with her "reading-for-fun" process, see the box on the next page. You will no doubt notice that her strategies combine idiosyncratic habits (the blue pen and cold room) with sound, widely used academic reading habits (looking over chapter headings, checking for study guide questions, and so on).

What personal habits or rituals do you combine with your more purposeful reading behaviors? The awareness and flexibility evident in the way Sheri talks about her reading are valuable because planning as she does would enable you to work efficiently and maximize the use of your time. Furthermore, thinking about your purpose as Sheri does will help you maintain a sense of your own authority as you read, a notion that is very important for college writing.

Sheri's self-awareness and deliberate reading strategies are not typical. When we ask students to describe the behaviors of good readers, many initially say "speed" or "the ability to understand a text in a single reading." Surprisingly, most experienced readers don't aim for speed reading, nor do they report that reading is an easy, one-step process. On the contrary, experienced readers put considerable effort into reading and rereading a text, adapting their strategies and speed to its demands and to their purpose for reading. Because your purposes for reading academic assignments will vary considerably, so must your academic reading strategies. You will read much differently, for example, if your task is to interpret or analyze a text than if you are simply skimming it for its potential usefulness in a research project. Contrary to popular myth, expert readers are not necessarily "speed" readers. Experienced readers pace themselves according to their purpose, taking advantage of four basic reading speeds:

- *Very fast:* Readers scan a text very quickly if they are looking only for a specific piece of information.

PREPARING TO READ: SHERI'S PROCESS

"When I am reading for class, for starters I make sure that I have all of my reading supplies. These include my glasses, a highlighter, pencil, blue pen, notebook paper, dictionary, and a quiet place to read, which has a desk or table. (It also has to be cold!) Before I read for class or for research purposes I always look over chapter headings or bold print words and then formulate questions based on these. When I do this it helps me to become more interested in the text I am reading because I am now looking for answers.

"Also, if there are study guide questions, I will look them over so that I have a basic idea of what to look for. I will then read the text all the way through, find the answers to my questions, and underline all of the study guide answers in pencil.

"When I read for fun, it's a whole other story! I always take off my shoes and sit on the floor/ground or in a very comfortable chair. I always prefer to read in natural light and preferably fresh air. I just read and relax and totally immerse myself in the story or article or whatever!"[4]

- *Fast:* Readers skim a text rapidly if they are trying to get just the general gist without worrying about details.
- *Slow to moderate:* Readers read carefully in order to get complete understanding of an article. The more difficult the text, the more slowly they read. Often difficult texts require rereading.
- *Very slow:* Experienced readers read very slowly if their purpose is to analyze a text. They take elaborate marginal notes and often pause to ponder over the construction of a paragraph or the meaning of an image or metaphor. Sometimes they reread the text dozens of times.

As your expertise grows within the fields you study, you will undoubtedly learn to vary your reading speed and strategies according to your purposes, even to the point of considering "efficient" reading of certain texts to involve slowing way down and rereading.

How Expert Readers Use Rhetorical Knowledge to Read Efficiently

This section illustrates two strategies used by expert readers to apply rhetorical knowledge to their reading processes.

---

[4]Sheri's description of her reading process is quoted in Paula Gillespie and Neal Lerner, *The Allyn and Bacon Guide to Peer Tutoring* (Boston: Allyn & Bacon, 2000), 105. Print.

Using Genre Knowledge to Read Efficiently

Besides varying reading speed to match their purpose, experienced readers also adjust their reading strategies to match the genre of a text. It is clear that the articles represented in Figures 2.2 and 2.3 (pp. 24–25) call for different kinds of reading strategies, but you may be surprised to learn that many scientists wouldn't read the scholarly article straight through from beginning to end. Instead, depending on their purpose, it is likely that they would read different sections in different order. The material in the following box describes how a group of physicists were guided both by their purpose for reading and by their familiarity with the genre conventions of scientific research reports. We invite you to read the material in the box before proceeding to the next paragraph.

Considering how scientists with different interests read specialized articles in their discipline, we can surmise that some researchers would read the results section of the *Appetite* article very carefully, whereas others would concentrate on the methodology section. Still another reader, perhaps a graduate student interested in finding a dissertation topic, might read it to see what research the authors say still needs to be accomplished. With sharply narrow interests and purposes, these readers would probably not find the article difficult to read. In contrast, nonspecialists might find it daunting to read, but as experienced readers, they would recognize that it is not necessary to understand all the details in order to understand the article's gist. They might read the abstract, then skip directly to the discussion section, where the authors analyze the meaning and the significance of their results.

PHYSICISTS' TECHNIQUES FOR EFFICIENT READING

Researchers who studied the way that physicists read articles in physics journals found that the physicists seldom read the article from beginning to end but instead used their knowledge of the typical structure of scientific articles to find the information most relevant to their interests. Scientific articles typically begin with an abstract or summary of their contents. The main body of these articles includes a five-part structure: (1) an introduction that describes the research problem, (2) a review of other studies related to this problem, (3) a description of the methodology used in the research, (4) a report of the results, and (5) the conclusions drawn from the results. The physicists in the study read the abstracts first to see if an article was relevant to their own research. If it was, the experimental physicists went to the methodology section to see if the article reported any new methods. By contrast, the theoretical physicists went to the results section to see if the article reported any significant new results.[5]

---

[5]Research reported by Cheryl Geisler, *Academic Literacy and the Nature of Expertise* (Hillsdale, NJ: Erlbaum, 1994), 20–21. Print.

Using a Text's Social/Historical Context to Make Predictions and Ask Questions

Recognizing that a text is part of a larger conversation about a particular topic, experienced readers can also use textual cues—such as format, style, and terminology—as well as their own background knowledge to speculate about the original context of a text, make predictions about it, and formulate questions.

These strategies for actively engaging with a text's social or historical context are illustrated in Ann Feldman's report of interviews with expert readers reading texts within their own areas of expertise. For example, Professor Lynn Weiner, a social historian, describes in detail her behind-the-scenes thinking as she prepared to read a chapter entitled "From the Medieval to the Modern Family" from Philippe Aries's *Centuries of Childhood: A Social History of Family Life*, written in 1962. Quotations from Professor Weiner's description of her thinking are shown in the box below. As Professor Weiner reads, she continues to elaborate this context, confirming and revising predictions, asking new questions, evaluating what Aries has to say in light of the evidence he can provide, and assessing the value of his ideas to her own work as a social historian. She concludes by saying, "A path-breaking book, it was credited with advancing the idea that childhood as a stage of life is historically constructed and not the same in every culture and every time. In my own work I might refer to Aries as I think and write about families as they exist today."

Professor Weiner's description of creating a context for understanding the Aries book suggests that the ability to recognize what you do not know and to raise questions about a text is as important as identifying what you do know and understand. Sometimes readers can reconstruct context from external clues such as a title and headings; from a text's visual appearance; from background

BUILDING A CONTEXT FOR READING

"This work isn't precisely in my field and it is a difficult text. I also know it by its reputation. But, like any student, I need to create a context in which to understand this work. When the book was written, the idea of studying the family was relatively new. Before this time historians often studied kings, presidents, and military leaders. That's why this new type of social history encouraged us to ask, 'How did ordinary people live?' Not the kings, but the families in the middle ages. Then we have to ask: 'Which families is [Aries] talking about? What causes the change that he sees? . . . For whom is the change significant?' . . . I'll want to be careful not . . . to assume the old family is bad and the new family is good. The title suggests a transition so I'll be looking for signs of it."[6]

---

[6]Ann Feldman, *Writing and Learning in the Disciplines* (New York: Harper, 1996), 16–17, 25–29. Print.

notes about the author, including the date and place of publication; or from what a book's table of contents reveals about its structure and scope. But readers often have to rely on internal evidence to get a full picture. A text's context and purpose may become evident through some quick spot reading (explained in the next chapter), especially in the introduction and conclusion. Sometimes, however, the full rhetorical and social context can be reconstructed only through a great deal of puzzling as you read. It's not unusual that a whole first reading is needed to understand exactly what conversation the writer is joining and how she or he intends to affect that conversation. Once that context becomes clear, rereading of key passages will make the text easier to comprehend.

Typical Reading-Based Writing Assignments Across the Curriculum

In college, a reading assignment is often only the first step in a complex series of activities that lead toward writing something that will be graded. In many cases, the material you are asked to read and respond to may include visual elements that demand attention, such as charts and graphs, photographs, drawings, or specific features of document or Web design. What you write will naturally vary according to the situation, ranging from a quick answer on an essay exam to an extensive source-based paper. In this section, we discuss five types of common college assignments in which reading plays a major role:

1. Writing to understand course content more fully
2. Writing to report your understanding of what a text says
3. Writing to practice the conventions of a particular type of text
4. Writing to make claims about a text
5. Writing to extend the conversation

The role that reading plays in connection with these different purposes for writing can be placed along a continuum, starting at one end with assignments in which the ideas in the texts you read predominate and moving to assignments in which the content is subordinate to your own ideas and aims. The first two assignment types ask you to write in order to learn course subject matter and to practice careful listening to texts. The last three ask you to compose your own analyses and arguments for specific audiences. Writing teachers sometimes distinguish these two categories of assignment goals by referring to them as "writing to learn" and "learning to write."

Writing to Understand Course Content More Fully

"Writing-to-learn" assignments aim to deepen your understanding of materials you read by asking you to put the author/creator's ideas into your own words or to identify points of confusion for yourself. The primary audience for writing in this category is often yourself, although teachers may sometimes ask you to submit them so that they can check on your understanding and progress. The style is informal and conversational. Organization and grammatical correctness are less important than the quality of your engagement with the content of the reading. These assignments typically take one of the following forms.

In-Class Freewriting

The point of freewriting is to think rapidly without censoring your thoughts. It is often assigned in class as a way to stimulate thinking about the day's subject. A typical in-class freewrite assignment might be this:

> Choose what for you personally is the single most important word in what we read for today. You need not speculate about which word the author or your instructor or any other classmate would choose. Just choose the word that seems most important to you, and then explore in writing why you chose it. This word may occur only once or many times.[7]

Reading or Learning Logs

Reading or learning logs are informal assignments, usually organized chronologically, in which you record your understanding, questions, and responses to a reading or image. Some teachers give specific prompts for entries, whereas others just ask that you write them with a certain regularity and/or of a certain length. A typical prompt might be "How would you describe the author's voice in this essay?" If a teacher asks you simply to write your own reflections in a log, you might use some of the questions rhetorical readers ask (pp. 10–11) to examine the text's method and your response to it.

Double-Entry Journals

Double-entry journals are like reading logs but formatted so that you may conduct an ongoing dialogue with your own interpretations and reactions to a text. Once again, the audience is primarily yourself. Although the double-entry system was originally designed for lined notebook paper, it can work equally well—or even better—on screen. Here is how the system works: Divide a notebook page with a line down the middle, or set up a two-column layout in your word processing program. On the right side of the page, record reading notes—direct quotations, observations, comments, questions, objections. On the left side, record your later reflections about those notes—second thoughts, responses to quotations, reactions to earlier comments, answers to questions or new questions. Skip lines as necessary so that your dialogue on the left lines up with your original notes on the right. Another option is to use a commenting function to create a sidebar column for your responses to your original notes; but in our experience, students find the spatial alignment difficult to track. Rhetorician Ann Berthoff, who popularized the double-entry approach, says that it

---

[7]We thank Joan Ruffino, an instructor at the University of Wisconsin–Milwaukee, for this freewriting assignment.

provides readers with a means of conducting a "continuing audit of meaning."[8] In a double-entry journal, you carry on a conversation with yourself about a text.

Short Thought Pieces or Postings to a Discussion Board

Sometimes written for an instructor, sometimes for a specified group of peers, short (250–300 words) response papers or "thought" pieces are somewhat more formal than the assignments discussed so far, but they are still much more informal than essay assignments. They call for a fuller response than the previous types of writing, but the purpose is similar—to articulate an understanding of a particular text by identifying significant points and offering a personal response or interpretation of them. Teachers will often provide a specific prompt for these assignments, sometimes as a way to generate a series of short pieces that will build to a larger paper. When the piece is written for a discussion forum, instructors may ask that you include a question or respond to a classmate's questions.

Here is a sample response piece that was posted to an online class forum. The teacher asked the students to write about the insights they gleaned regarding obsessive-compulsive disorder (OCD) from reading Lauren Slater's essay "Black Swans," in which the author narrates the onset of her ongoing battle with it.

Student Posting to a Class Forum

Reading "Black Swans" taught me some basic information about OCD, but more importantly, it taught me how terrifying this disease can be. It begins with a single obsessive thought that leads to a cycle of anxiety, repetitive behaviors, and avoidance of situations that produce the obsessive thoughts. In severe cases, like Slater's, the person completely avoids life because the obsessive thoughts invade every aspect of life.

What impressed me most about this essay, however, was Slater's ability to put me in her shoes and make me feel some of the terror she felt. She vividly describes her experience at being stricken with this condition without warning. A single thought—"I can't concentrate"—suddenly blocked out all other thoughts. Even her own body seemed foreign to her and grotesque: "the phrase 'I can't concentrate on my hand' blocked out my hand, so all I saw was a blur of flesh giving way to the bones beneath, and inside the bones the grimy marrow, and in the grimy marrow the individual cells, all disconnected." I see why Max says it was the most terrifying aspect of the disease to him. I can't imagine being disconnected from my own body. More horrifying to me, though, was her sense of being completely unable to control her mind: "My mind was devouring my mind." I will be interested to see what others think.

---

[8]Ann Berthoff, *The Making of Meaning* (Montclair, NJ: Boynton Cook, 1981), 45. Print.

Writing to Report Your Understanding of What a Text Says

Another common reading-based assignment asks you to report your understanding of what a text says. Here, your goal is to summarize the text rather than respond to it. Reports like this are necessary, for example, when essay exam questions ask students to contrast the ideas of several authors. Another example would be an **annotated bibliography** summarizing sources related to a particular topic or question, or a literature review at the beginning of a report for a science class. A summary can be as short as a single sentence (when, for example, you want to provide context for a quotation in a paper) or longer and more detailed (when, for example, you are summarizing an opposing view that you intend to refute in your own argument.) Although summaries or reports of your understanding of a text will vary in length and purpose, they are always expected to be accurate, fair, and balanced. (We offer guidelines for writing summaries for a variety of purposes, including a rhetorical précis, in Chapter 3.)

Writing to Practice the Conventions of a Particular Type of Text

Assignments that ask you to practice the conventions of a particular type of writing—its organizational format, style, ways of presenting evidence, and so on—use readings as models. Such assignments are common in college courses. In a journalism class, for example, you would learn to write a news report using the inverted pyramid structure; in a science course, you would learn to write up the results of a lab experiment in a particular scientific report format. Novices in a discipline learn to write in specialized genres by reading examples and practicing their formats and rhetorical "moves."

Generally, using readings as models of a genre or subgenre involves the following activities:

- Identifying the features that characterize a particular type of text
- Noting the ways in which a rhetorical situation affects the features identified in model texts
- Deciding on your own topic and reason for writing this particular type of text
- Using the features of the model text (or texts) and your own rhetorical situation to guide your writing

Let's say, for example, that you've been asked to write a **proposal argument**. Proposals typically include three main features: description of the problem, proposal of a solution, and justification of that solution. As you read sample proposals, you will find that in different contexts, authors deal with these features differently, depending on their audience and purpose. In some cases, for example, there is a great deal of description of the problem because the intended audience is unfamiliar with it or doesn't recognize it as a problem. In other cases, it is presumed that the intended reading audience already recognizes the problem. The key to success is to adapt a model text's structural and stylistic characteristics to your own rhetorical purpose, not to follow the model slavishly. (For more details about proposal arguments, see Table 2.1 on pp. 19–20.)

In courses across the curriculum, your ability to analyze and adopt the conventions particular to a given discipline's ways of writing will help you write successful papers. For example, when you are asked in a philosophy class to write an argument in response to Immanuel Kant's *Critique of Pure Reason,* you are primarily being asked to engage with the ideas in the text. But secondarily, you are also being asked to practice the conventions of writing a philosophical argument in which counterexamples and counterarguments are expected. Thus, in any field of study, it pays to be alert not only to the ideas presented in material you are assigned to read, but also to its structure and style.

Writing to Make Claims About a Text

Assignments in this category ask you to analyze and critique texts, including texts in which images and layout are key elements of rhetorical effect. Such papers must go beyond a summary of what a text says to make claims about that content and how it is presented. Many academic writers take as their field of study the texts produced by others. Literary critics study novels, poems, and plays; cultural critics analyze song lyrics, advertisements, cereal boxes, and television scripts; historians analyze primary source documents from the past; theologians scrutinize the sacred texts of different religions; lawyers analyze the documents entered into court proceedings, the exact wording of laws and statutes, and the decisions of appellate courts. In all these cases, the analysis and critique involve examining small parts of the whole to understand, explain, and perhaps object to, overall points and success.

Many college composition courses ask students to write rhetorical analyses of texts. To **analyze**—a word that at its root means "take apart"—a text, you need to identify specific rhetorical methods and strategies used by the author, show how these rhetorical choices contribute to the text's impact, and evaluate those elements in light of the author's evident purpose. In assignments like this, the text and your ideas about it are of equal importance. These assignments asking for analysis are not invitations for you to refer briefly to the text and then take off on your own opinions about the topic, nor are they invitations merely to summarize or rehearse what the text has said. Rather, analysis assignments expect you to engage critically with a specific text. On the one hand, you will be expected to represent what the text said accurately and fairly. On the other hand, you will be expected to offer your own analysis, interpretation, or critique in a way that enables readers to see the text differently. Further guidance about engaging with texts this way appears in Chapter 4, which includes guidelines for writing a rhetorical analysis along with a sample assignment and student paper as illustration.

Writing to Extend the Conversation

These assignments treat texts as voices in a conversation about ideas. They typically ask writers to read and synthesize material from several sources. Here, your own ideas and aims take center stage; your source texts play important but less prominent backup roles. The most familiar form this assignment takes is the research or seminar paper. A key difference between these assignments and high school research papers is that college instructors expect the paper to present your own argument, not simply to report what others have said. In other words, you are expected to articulate a significant question or problem, research what published authors have said about it in print or on the Web, and formulate your own argument. To write these multisource papers successfully, you must use your source texts primarily to position yourself in the conversation and to supply supporting data, information, or testimony. The argument—your main points—must come from you.

A helpful way to approach these assignments is to treat the texts you have read as springboards for further research and discovery. Think of the readings you encounter in your research as voices in a conversation that your essay will join. By giving you the opportunity to define your own purposes for writing in dialog with other texts, such assignments prepare you for the research assignments typical of many college courses, where your goal is to synthesize material from a number of sources and then produce your own paper, inserting another voice—your own—into the ongoing conversation. To illustrate this kind of research writing, at the end of Chapter 6 we include Jack's analysis of multiple perspectives on the potential of corn ethanol as an automobile fuel.

Chapter Summary

This chapter has focused on the three major elements of rhetorical context—purpose, audience, and genre. In the first part of the chapter, we explained how to analyze these three factors for a text that you are reading. We then showed you how to analyze your own rhetorical context as a reader/writer. In particular, we showed you how

- To analyze a text's original rhetorical context
- To determine your own rhetorical context and to match your reading strategies to your own purposes
- To use rhetorical knowledge to make your reading more efficient
  - By using genre knowledge to read more efficiently
  - By analyzing the text's original social/historical context

Finally, we explained five different ways that assignments across the curriculum might ask you to use readings.

Listening to a Text

The process of reading is not just the interpretation of a text but the interpretation of another person's worldview as presented by a text.

—Doug Brent

I n this chapter, we focus specifically on the nuts and bolts of reading the kinds of texts you will be assigned in college. You will learn to integrate the strategies used by experienced readers into your own reading repertoire. These strategies—for **preparing to read, reading initially, and rereading**—will make you both a better reader and a shrewder writer.

Our discussion in this chapter as well as the next extends the metaphor of reading as conversation by using the terms "listening" and "questioning" to describe specific reading techniques. The **listening strategies** we discuss will help you read attentively so that you can understand a text in the way the author intended and then represent the text fairly when you write about it.

To illustrate the strategies presented in the rest of this chapter and in Chapter 4, we will refer to three texts: the *UC Berkeley Wellness Letter* article, "Chew on This," found on page 25; an excerpt from art historian Kirk Savage's chapter

---

In this chapter, you will learn

- Strategies that will help you attend closely to a text and give it the fairest hearing possible
- Concepts for "reading" visual elements and recognizing how they enhance, support, or extend points contained in a verbal text
- Techniques for preparing idea maps and descriptive outlines of texts (both verbal and visual)
- Guidelines for composing summaries and rhetorical précis.

on the Vietnam Veterans Memorial in *Monument Wars*, "The Conscience of the Nation," printed at the end of this chapter; and Atul Gawande's argument for "A Life-Saving Checklist," presented at the end of Chapter 4. We use "Chew on This" as an example of the lively popular pieces you are likely to encounter when doing research on contemporary culture. Savage's text illustrates the sophisticated scholarly reading you are likely to be assigned in a variety of disciplines. Gawande's text exemplifies the tightly argued opinion pieces you will find when you research public policy issues or when you read news and opinion articles in the ordinary course of being an informed citizen.

Writing as You Read

Rhetorical readers "listen" by reading with pen in hand in order to interact with the text and record their ideas-in-progress. When they read on screen, they use a text highlight tool or keep a second file open for note-taking. You will find that writing as you read will transform your reading process from passive receptivity into active meaning-making.

You may have heard of "active listening," a technique by which listeners use eye contact and body language to convey that they are listening carefully to someone. Writing as you read is **active reading**. Skilled rhetorical readers might write in the margins of a text (unless it is a library book), or they might keep a reading log or journal in which they record notes—on paper or in a designated "ideas" file on their computer. Sometimes they stop reading in the middle of a passage and freewrite their ideas-in-progress. When a text stimulates their own thinking, writing down those ideas captures that thinking for future reference and stimulates further thought. To put it another way, rhetorical reading strategies focus on both **comprehension** (a reader's understanding of a text) and **invention**—the ideas a reader generates in response to a text. Thus, writing while you read helps you generate ideas, as well as interact more deeply with a text.

Not surprisingly, then, most of the rhetorical reading strategies that we present in this book require you to write. To foster the reading-writing connection, we recommend that you, too, keep a reading log, paper or electronic, in which you practice the strategies described in this chapter. Doing so will help you develop powerful advanced reading skills, as well as generate a wealth of ideas for essay topics.

Depending on your purposes for reading a given text, some of the strategies described in this chapter will seem more appropriate in some situations than in others. Some are used consciously by experienced readers on a regular basis; others are designed to help you acquire the mental habits that have become second nature to experienced readers. For example, they almost always take notes as they read, and they frequently write summaries of what they have read. However, experienced readers would be less likely to write a descriptive outline (described later in this chapter; see pp. 56–59), not because the exercise isn't valuable, but because experience has allowed them to internalize the mental habit of attending to both the content and function of paragraphs as they read.

By practicing descriptive outlining on a couple of readings, you too will begin to internalize this dual focus of rhetorical reading. Descriptive outlining is also a valuable tool to use in your own writing as you analyze a draft in order to make decisions about revision. In addition, it will foster your ability to talk about visuals—how they work, and how you might use them in your own writing.

Preparing to Read

In Chapters 1 and 2, we pointed out that strong readers manage their reading processes according to the type of text they are reading and their purpose for reading it. The strategies we present in this section encourage you to prepare to read as though you were about to join the text in a multi-voiced conversation. As we explained in Chapter 1, the text you are reading is one voice among a network of other voices. Your response to the text constitutes yet another voice in the ongoing conversation about the topic. Practicing these strategies will prepare you to read in a powerful way that will enable you to join that conversation.

Recalling Background Knowledge

By pausing to recall your prior knowledge, experience, and opinions regarding a text's subject matter, you can make your reading more purposeful. As illustration, recall for a moment the sociology assignment we imagined in Chapter 2: an annotated bibliography on a controversy over the effects of pop culture on family values (pp. 27–28). Before you begin reading, it might be helpful to narrow the scope of your research by considering what aspects of "pop culture" have, in your experience, seemed most objectionable to defenders of "family values." Still more important for careful reading would be to define for yourself the term "family values" so that you can track your ideas against the way the term is used in the materials you find. Your sociology textbook might offer a standard definition, for example, or you might find several articles with consistent definitions. On the other hand, if you found that writers are at odds about how to define the term, that controversy would be very important to note and track.

For any assignment, pausing to review your background knowledge will help you recognize the gaps in that knowledge. By jotting down some notes about what you know and need to know, you can establish benchmarks that will help you assess a text's effect on your current views or beliefs, as well as its usefulness for a writing project. The journals or reading logs that we recommend are the perfect place to brainstorm about what you already know or feel about a subject. If you have little knowledge about the subject, jot down some questions that will enable you to engage with what you read. Leave open the possibility that your ideas and purposes for writing might change as you read. Later, when you finish reading the text, the notes in your reading log will provide valuable cues for review.

As you jot reading notes and review them, ask yourself questions like these:

- What did I learn from the text that is new to me?
- What did the text prompt me to consider that I had not thought about before?
- Has the text confirmed my prior knowledge and beliefs—or has it raised some doubts?
- How might I use information and ideas from this text when I write papers or exams, or make decisions in my workplace or community?

Using Visual Elements to Plan and Predict

Visual features are one of the first things we notice about a text. They lead us to approach the reading of a poem, for example, quite differently than we do the reading of a scholarly article, résumé, or comic strip. Even tacit knowledge of genres sets up particular expectations and affects how we go about reading a text. As we point out in Chapter 2's discussion of genre, the design of a text, on paper or screen, provides important clues to its writer's and publisher's designs upon readers' attention and ideas. The color, design, and images on a book or magazine cover typically are meant to entice us to open and read inside. On Web sites, color, design, images, and animation combine to grab our attention so that we'll pause to read instead of clicking away to a new page. Textbooks capitalize on color and page design to hold and guide students' attention. Careful attention to a text's visual features can help you plan your reading of it, as well as enable you to make predictions about its purpose. It is common practice for students to leaf through a textbook chapter to spot illustrations, charts, or graphs; to note the headings on subsections; and, of course, to calculate how long it will take to read an assigned set of pages.

Although it may seem that the visual features of a text are distinct from the verbal, the print features of written texts also affect readers' attitudes and expectations about a reading. Broadly, it is inevitable that we take in the layout of pages and screens we encounter, perhaps without attending specifically to the details assembled by the page designers. Readers notice images, especially large ones, accompanying a text, and as we discuss later in this chapter and the next, these images inevitably influence our understanding and appreciation of the contents. Indeed, even the absence of images has an impact, as in the text-heavy page of the scholarly journal seen in Figure 2.2 (p. 24). At a more fine-grained level, the choice of typeface and font size can affect not only readability, but the way a text conveys a mood and tone. Consider the different levels of seriousness and informality conveyed by the fonts in Figure 3.1. These differences are significant for your choices as a writer because just as they help you recognize context and purpose when you read various textual genres, they provide

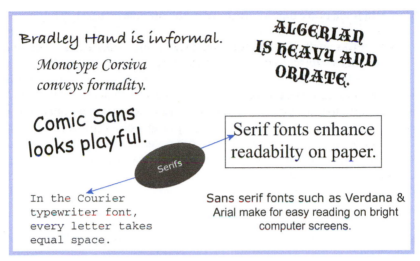

FIGURE 3.1 Typeface varieties

the same signals to your own readers. For example, we have all been cautioned against using ALL CAPS in emails because they give the effect of SHOUTING. Similarly, it is wise to submit academic papers printed in a typeface, or font, that has **serifs**, those little strokes at the tops and bottoms of letters. Doing so will make your paper easier for your professors to read and will convey the message that you are aware of appropriate academic conventions.

Consider the visual features of this chapter: frequent subheadings, bold-faced terms, bulleted lists, annotated examples. What do these features suggest about its genre? About how to go about reading it? Even if you were reading a copy of this chapter on screen or on paper separately from the book, you would easily recognize that it came from a textbook because its instructional features emphasize important points and break up information for ease of reading and review. Because you are quite familiar with textbooks, you have undoubtedly developed strategies for reading texts like this one—skimming the headings before reading, noting words in bold, using the bulleted information for review.

Spot Reading

Spot reading is a process that gives you a quick overview of a text's content and structure and thus helps you (a) determine the fit of the text's rhetorical context and purpose with your own purposes for reading; and (b) predict content and formulate questions. For example, when your purpose for reading is to acquaint yourself with the vocabulary and concepts of a new field, spot reading will help you determine whether a book or article is written at an introductory level. If it is, then you can expect textual cues to point to important new vocabulary and concepts. If it is not, then you may decide to find a more basic introductory text to read first, or you may decide to look up unfamiliar terms and to allot extra time to reread passages that seem dense initially.

If an article or book that interests you has an abstract or introduction, you might begin spot reading there. Other places for productive spot reading are the opening and concluding paragraphs or sections of an article. The opening usually introduces subject matter and announces a purpose, and the conclusion often sums up the text's major ideas. If you are working with a textbook that provides summaries and study questions, it is a good idea to read through these before beginning to read the section they describe. If the text is short, you might try reading the opening sentences of each paragraph. With a book, consider what the chapter titles in the table of contents reveal. Sometimes, particularly in textbooks, the table of contents will provide subheadings that reveal valuable detail about content. Spot reading there can help you determine what will be covered and whether the book, or particular parts of it, will help you address a research question. Furthermore, the organizational strategy revealed through a table of contents can provide important information about an author's method, perhaps guiding you to choose certain sections as essential reading.

An Extended Example: Spot Reading in Kirk Savage's *Monument Wars*

Suppose you are enrolled in a Humanities seminar focused on public art and are part of a small group putting together a print- and Web-based research project related to Vietnam and other war memorials in your group members' various hometowns as well as in Washington, D.C. (A photo of the Vietnam Veterans Memorial in Washington is presented in Figure 3.2.) Imagine that your professor has recommended that you "read around" in a book by Kirk Savage called *Monument Wars*. When you look up the library call number, you learn that it was published fairly recently (2009) by an academic press (University of California Press), and you glean valuable insights about content from its

FIGURE 3.2 Visitors at the national Vietnam Veterans Memorial in Washington, D.C. Visitors often pause to create rubbings of names engraved into the reflective black stone. The two intersecting walls memorialize more than 58,000 members of the U.S. Armed Forces who were killed or missing in action in Southeast Asia between 1959 and 1975, or who died later from injuries directly related to combat in the Vietnam War.

FIGURE 3.3 Illustration of Maya Lin's winning design for the Vietnam Veterans Memorial, by Paul Oles, 1981

subtitle: *Washington, D.C., the National Mall, and the Transformation of the Memorial Landscape.* These signs of the book's scholarly credentials give substance to your professor's recommendation. Furthermore, when you find it on the library shelf you discover that it is heavy and thick—390 pages—many of them devoted to notes, a bibliography, and an index. A serious book. Will it be difficult to read? Are you part of its intended audience?

Flipping through the pages on your way to the circulation desk, you would see that the book has many photographs and other illustrations directly related to the Vietnam Veterans Memorial (VVM), including the one reproduced in Figure 3.3. Back at the front of the book, you might notice the author's dedication of the book to his family and, curiously, "to all the people of this earth who may never have a monument to call their own." Thus the author sets a tone that runs counter to the book's many images of ornate buildings and heroes on horseback. Although details about the author are scarce in the book itself, a quick Web search later will reveal that Kirk Savage holds a high academic position at the University of Pittsburgh and writes frequently in a personal blog about war memorials and monuments. "A great potential resource," you might think as you sit down to examine the book itself.

Consider the list of chapter titles on the Contents page:

1. A Monument to a Deceased Project
2. Covering Ground
3. The Mechanic Monster
4. Inventing Public Space

---

[1] An excerpt from this chapter appears on pages 65–68.
[2] Kirk Savage, *Monument Wars* (Berkeley, CA: U California P, 2009). N. pag.

While the term "public space" in the title of Chapter 4 would echo concepts discussed in your class, the idea of "the monument transformed" or a monument serving as the "conscience of the nation" would be highly intriguing. A closer look at the illustrations during another flip through the pages reveals that the book is organized chronologically. A quick skim of the introduction confirms the dedication's hint that Savage is interested in the human side of memorials. He begins by quoting a congressman from 1800 to the effect that the invention of the printing press has made monuments "good for nothing" (1), something Savage obviously intends to dispute. Spot reading of the opening sentences of the paragraphs that follow underscores the subtitle's suggestion that the history of monuments on the National Mall is one of disputes and conflicts. Savage begins the final paragraph of the introduction this way: "All this means that monuments will still be subject to dispute and change before and after they are built, and the landscape of national memory will never cease to evolve" (22).

A quick check of the index reveals quite a few pages listed under "Vietnam Veterans Memorial," so you would likely leave the library confident that you have an excellent resource, one you can not only "read around" in but use for ideas directly relevant to your project. You might even decide to buy your own copy so that you can mark it up as you read.

As this example shows, spot reading can provide a framework for making predictions and posing questions about content that will help you make sense of ideas and information once you begin reading. It can also help you anticipate and tolerate difficult-to-understand passages, confident that, even though you don't understand every bit of the text on the first reading, you nevertheless have some sense of its overall purpose. In short, spot reading helps you stay in control of your reading process by helping you confirm and revise your predictions and look for answers to your questions. It takes little time and offers a worthwhile payoff in increased understanding.

Listening as You Read Initially

Just as good listeners attend carefully to what their conversational partners say, trying to give them a fair hearing, so, too, do good readers "listen" carefully to what a text says, trying to consider its ideas carefully and accurately before rushing to judgment. College reading assignments put a particular premium on giving an impartial hearing to ideas and positions that are new and sometimes radically different from your own. Moreover, in class discussions, examinations, and paper assignments, you will frequently be asked to demonstrate that you have listened well to assigned texts. Professors want to know that you have comprehended these texts with reasonable accuracy before you proceed to analyze, apply, or critique the ideas in them. In the language of Kenneth Burke's metaphor of the conversational parlor, you might think of this listening phase of the reading process as the phase where you try to catch the drift of the conversation and give it the fullest and fairest hearing before "putting in your oar."

Listening strategies help you understand what to listen for, how to hear what the text is saying, and how to track your evolving understanding of the text. The first time through a text, reading with its grain, you are trying to understand a text's overall gist and compose a "rough-draft interpretation" of its meaning and your own response. As we discuss later in this chapter, after you have a sense of the gist, a second reading will enable you to confirm and deepen your understanding, and revise it if necessary.

We have urged you to read with a pen or pencil in hand, to adopt experienced readers' practice of marking passages, drawing arrows, and making notes. (You can do this with electronic highlighting and annotating, too.) Active use of your hands as well as your eyes will be necessary to undertake the four strategies for an efficient initial reading that we recommend in the next four sections.

Note Organizational Signals

Headings and transition words serve as organizational signals that help you anticipate and then track a text's overall structure of ideas. Experienced readers use these signals to identify the text's central ideas, to distinguish major ideas from minor ones, to anticipate what is coming next, and to determine the relationship among the text's major ideas. Organizational signals and forecasting statements (which directly tell you what to expect) function like road signs, giving you information about direction, upcoming turns, and the distance yet to go. For example, experienced readers note words that signal a change in the direction of thought, such as *however, in contrast,* or *on the other hand.* Likewise, they take advantage of the guidance provided by words such as *first, second,* and *third* that signal a series of parallel points or ideas; words such as *therefore, consequently,* or *as a result* that signal logical relationships; and words such as *similarly, also,* or *likewise* that signal additional support for the current point. Circling or otherwise marking these terms will make it possible for a quick glance back to remind you of the structure of ideas.

Mark Unfamiliar Terms and References

As you read, it is important to mark unfamiliar terms and references because they offer contextual clues about the intended audience and the conversation of which a given text is a part. The very unfamiliarity of these terms and references may tell you that the text is written for an insider audience whose members share a particular kind of knowledge and concerns. To become part of the conversation, you need to learn such terms. We suggest that you mark them with a question mark or write them in the margins and return to them after you finish your initial reading. Stopping to look them up as you read will break your concentration. By looking them up later, after you have that "rough-draft" sense of the text's overall purpose, you will gain insight into how key terms function and how they represent major concerns of a particular field or area of study.

"Read as though it made sense and perhaps it will."

—I. A. Richards

Identify Points of Difficulty

One of the most important traits of experienced readers is probably their *tolerance for ambiguity and initial confusion*. They have learned to read through points of difficulty, trusting that confusing points will become clear as they continue to read. When you are reading about new and difficult subject matter, you will inevitably encounter passages that you simply do not understand. A valuable reading strategy is to identify explicitly what you don't understand. We recommend that you bracket puzzling passages and keep reading. Later, you can come back to them and try to translate them into your own words or to frame questions about them to ask your classmates and professor.

Annotate

When you annotate a text, you underline, highlight, draw arrows, and make marginal comments. Annotating is a way of making the text your own, of literally putting your mark on it—noting its key passages and ideas. Experienced readers rely on this common but powerful strategy to note reactions and questions, thereby recording their in-process understanding of a text. By marking the page, they are able to monitor their evolving construction of a text's meaning.

Annotations also serve a useful purpose when you return to a text to reread or review it. Not only can they remind you of your first impressions of the text's meaning, but they also can help you identify main points and come to new levels of understanding—clearer answers to earlier questions, new insights, and new questions. Indeed, we recommend that you annotate each time you read a text, perhaps using different colors so that you have a record of the new layers of meaning you discover. Of course, you would not do this in a library book, and there's one additional caveat: annotating can become counterproductive if you underline or highlight too enthusiastically. A completely underlined paragraph tells you nothing about its key point. To be useful, underlining must be selective, based both on your own purposes for reading and on what you think the writer's main points are. In general, when it is time to review the text and recall its main ideas, notes in the margin about main ideas, questions, objections, and connections will be far more useful than underlining or highlighting.

To illustrate this listening strategy, at the end of this chapter, we have annotated part of the excerpt from Kirk Savage's *Monument Wars* about the Vietnam Veterans Memorial on pages 65–68. The annotations were made from the perspective of the student we asked you to imagine who is working on a project about public art and memorials and who decided to buy a personal copy of the book in order to make annotations like these. These notes demonstrate one student's efforts to understand Savage's points about the memorial as an "antimonument." We invite you to turn to the selection now and read carefully through both the passage and the annotations. Consider how these or other annotations would help you understand the passage more fully—and think about what uses you or another student might make of these annotations.

Connecting the Visual to the Verbal

Visual images frequently accompany the verbal texts we encounter in periodicals and on the Web. They **enhance, support, and extend** a text's meaning, all in ways undoubtedly intended to increase rhetorical effectiveness. A number of factors work together to make the use of images particularly powerful. For one thing, we live in a highly visual culture where information is often transmitted through images. Our attention is more readily attracted and engaged by verbal texts that include visual elements. For another, the general beliefs persist not only that "a picture is worth a thousand words" but also that "pictures don't lie" and "seeing is believing," all despite widespread knowledge that images can easily be doctored or manipulated. (Indeed, puzzle quizzes about exactly how a photo has been changed have become popular in college newspapers.) For all of these reasons, careful readers must be alert to the subtle and indirect messages conveyed through visuals.

The importance of visual elements, particularly images, in relation to a text can vary considerably. At one end of the continuum are visual elements that are clearly incidental to the verbal message—for example, generic clip art added to a poster publicizing a meeting. At the other end are texts in which the visual message predominates and verbal elements play only a minor role, a phenomenon frequently seen in advertisements. Perhaps more significant at this end of the continuum are photographs of certain historical moments, images that have become iconic in that they have come to represent far more than the event recorded by the camera. Images of the planes ramming into the twin towers on September 11, 2001, come to mind as examples. An iconic historical image with a positive connotation features Dr. Martin Luther King, Jr., at the 1963 March on Washington. Photos from this event often show King at the Lincoln Memorial or the crowds stretching before him from the Reflecting Pool to the Washington Monument. They have come to stand not just for the event, or even progress toward the 1964 Civil Rights Act, but for Americans' freedom to peaceful assembly and protest.

Somewhere between incidental decorations and iconic historical images is the special case of cartoons, especially political cartoons. Here the visual and verbal are tightly intertwined, with the visual sometimes leading, sometimes carrying the verbal.

In academic writing, visual elements are usually subordinate to the verbal content, with their importance depending on their function. Nonetheless, it is very important that as an academic reader you stay alert to the way that visual elements function in relation to a verbal message and thus play into the rhetorical effect of a text.

Visuals That Enhance Verbal Content

Photographs, drawings, and other images often function to attract readers' attention, set a tone, and frame responses. In these ways, they **enhance** the text's verbal content by augmenting it with the vividness and immediacy of an image. The images of the Vietnam Veterans Memorial in Figures 3.2 and 3.3 here in this book on pages 44 and 45 function that way. Or consider the example of the colorful animated graphics that typically introduce television news programs, heralding station or network slogans about "late-breaking" or "leading-edge" news and "on-your-side" newscasters.

A survey of just a few campus bulletin boards will likely reveal multiple examples of visuals used primarily to enhance a textual message. A good example is prominently displayed in a classroom where one of us teaches. A photo of a young man's eyes and broad forehead take up almost all of an 11- by 17-inch poster. From across the room, the whites of his eyes and a jumble of print draw attention. The eyes are rolled way up, as if he is reading what is printed in several different sizes of type on his forehead. The largest print reads "62%," "regret," and "under." Walking closer, one can make out smaller type that reads, "the influence." (Are you guessing the topic at hand?) One must get very close to read the words in smallest print and thus put together the full message: "62% of students regret something they did under the influence of drugs and alcohol." Drawing us in to read that message is what that poster is all about. The big eyes and big forehead, while they might be read as symbolic of deep thought (or a headache), serve primarily as attention-getting enhancements of the message, which is part of a campaign against binge drinking designed to change ideas about what constitutes "normal" alcohol use on campus.

Visuals That Support Verbal Content

A second way in which the visual relates to the verbal, common especially in academic writing for technical and pre-professional fields, is to **support** the verbal message. In our everyday lives, news photographs offer a common example of how visual elements provide evidence for claims. The contrasting photographs in Figure 3.4, for example, document the destruction caused by Hurricane Sandy on a well-known amusement pier in Seaside Heights on the Jersey Shore. They thus provide dramatic background images for the Associated Press (AP) story they accompanied. The story, which the AP headlined "Will Jersey Shore ever be the same after Sandy?", celebrated the former iconic status of the boardwalk and the shoreline itself in American culture, and quoted local residents and celebrities lamenting the damage done and cherishing memories of the time spent at places like this.

FIGURE 3.4 Contrasting photographs of the Funtown Pier in Seaside Heights, New Jersey, before and after Hurricane Sandy in late October, 2012. The top photo was taken August 10, 2010, and the bottom on October 31, 2012.

Thanks to advances in computer software and printing technology, even student authors can provide evidence for their claims by referring readers directly to visual images in photographs and other graphics. Prominent among visual elements that support verbal content are **information graphics**, which

TABLE 3.1 • COMMON USES OF INFORMATION GRAPHICS	
Purpose	**Graphic to Use**
Present detailed or complex data	Table
Bring an object or process to life	Drawing, photograph, flowchart
Show change over time	Line graph
Show relation of parts to the whole	Pie chart
Contrast quantities and phenomena	Table, bar graph
Locate and show distribution of phenomena	Map
Highlight key points	Shaded boxes, bulleted lists

are typically used to promote readers' comprehension of discrete and detailed points of information, especially in workplace settings. Table 3.1 above—itself an information graphic—provides a quick list of visuals commonly used for specific explanatory and informative purposes. Most of these are fairly easy to create with standard desktop software, and are increasingly common in both print and Web materials.

Understanding the purpose and function of information graphics will help you develop your rhetorical reading skills and prepare you to incorporate graphic elements into your texts in college and on the job. Notice that the list of graphics in the right-hand column of Table 3.1 includes photographs and drawings, which become information graphics when they are used to support verbal material by providing illustration, typically with added captions. Similarly, elements of page design such as checklists, shaded boxes, and bulleted lists merge into this category when they are used to help readers efficiently find, use, and understand information.

Visuals That Extend Verbal Content

A third function visual elements can serve is to **extend** the meaning of a verbal text by enlarging or highlighting a particular dimension of it. Visual elements that function in this way can suggest new interpretations, provoke particular responses, or create links to other ideas. In many of these cases, a reader might initially puzzle over the connection between an image and the verbal text it accompanies, not knowing quite how to interpret it until after reading the text. Visuals that work this way often accompany advertisements, by implication connecting the product being sold with physical attractiveness, romantic success, improved economic status, or any number of other desirable attributes.

In some cases, a reader may not know quite how to interpret an image until after reading the text. Consider, for example, the drawing by Randy Mack Bishop in Figure 3.5. Bishop is an illustrator for the *Dallas Morning News* whose work is available to newspapers nationwide through NewsArt.com. Before we describe the context in which an editor at the *Milwaukee Journal Sentinel* placed it, take a moment to consider what ideas or issues Bishop's image evokes for you.

The drawing came to our attention when it appeared on the *Journal Sentinel*'s op-ed page alongside a reprinted opinion piece by *New York Times*

FIGURE 3.5 Editorial art drawing by Randy Mack Bishop

columnist Maureen Dowd with the headline "Scarred for Life: Courage Begets Courage."[3] Puzzled? We were. In the column, Dowd writes admiringly about her niece's courage in donating part of her liver to her uncle (Dowd's brother). By the end of the piece, Dowd has resolved to become an organ donor herself. Implicit in the column is an argument urging others to do the same. Because Bishop's drawing does not connect directly to the text, readers might interpret its meaning variously. However, most would probably agree that it extends Dowd's abstract idea of support, perhaps suggesting that the support of others enables us to be courageous and to rise above selfish concerns.

● FOR WRITING AND DISCUSSION

To explore the many different ways that visual elements of a text can connect to its verbal elements, work with a partner or group to examine how

---

[3]Maureen Dowd, "Scarred for Life: Courage Begets Courage," *Milwaukee Journal Sentinel* 3 June 2003: 11A. Published originally as "Our Own Warrior Princess," *New York Times* 1 June 2003: 4.13. Print.

the editors of a current print magazine have used various visual elements to engage readers. Prepare your findings for presentation to your classmates.

1. Focus on editorial content, not advertisements, to find examples of each role for visuals that we outline in this chapter.
2. Look for visuals that may serve more than one function. How do captions, if supplied, guide readers to connect them to verbal content?
3. Are there visuals that defy categorization? Explain.

For this assignment, we recommend examining both Web and paper issues of magazines available in most libraries that cover a variety of content for a broad, general audience, and that thus use many types of visuals, such as *Time, Bloomberg Business Week,* or *The New Yorker.* When you examine online editions of these periodicals, consider how various Web images compete with each other, then analyze how images function to draw the eye on the screen in contrast to on a print page.   •

Listening as You Reread

Rhetorical reading often requires careful rereading. Of course, not every text requires rereading; however, whenever detailed analysis is required or whenever a text is particularly difficult, a careful second (and sometimes a third) reading is needed. Experienced academic readers will often use the techniques we lay out in this section as a way of keeping track of complex texts that they will need to use as a basis for their own writing, perhaps as foundational evidence for their own assertions, perhaps as a taking-off point for a critique.

In the remainder of this chapter, to help you acquire the mental habits of strong academic readers and to give you practice with the types of writing you will use frequently as part of college-level analysis and research, we offer strategies for approaching texts in ways that go beyond skimming for content: idea maps, descriptive outlines, summaries, and rhetorical précis.

Mapping the Idea Structure

Idea maps provide a visual representation of a text's major ideas and the relationships among those ideas. In many college courses, it is important to get a sense of how an assigned text works as a whole, not just pieces of its concepts or data. An excellent way to establish this sense of the whole is to reread the text with the goal of creating an idea map. This process will enable you to distinguish main points from subordinate ones; then, as you connect them in a visual diagram, the process will help you understand how the text establishes relationships among those primary and secondary ideas. These relationships are akin to a hierarchy in a power structure: particular explanations and sets of details chunk together to support particular overarching points that in turn flesh out a thesis. You might think of idea maps as X-rays of the text's idea structure.

The time to map a text's idea structure is after you have finished reading it and are sitting back to review its main ideas. To create a map, draw a circle in the center of a page and write the text's main idea inside the circle. Then record the text's supporting ideas on branches and subbranches that extend from the center circle. In Figure 3.6, we offer a sample idea map of the excerpt from Savage's "The Conscience of the Nation," found on pages 65–68. If you tend not to be a visual thinker, creating an idea map can be challenging because it forces you to think about the text's main ideas in a new way; indeed, that is the advantage of doing an idea map. You may even find that creating a map reveals inconsistencies in the text's organizational structure or puzzling relationships among ideas. This, too, is important information and may be an issue you should bring up in class discussion or in your written responses to the text. In any case, creating an idea map is a way to understand a text at a deeper level and thus to understand and evaluate its importance in relation to course content or to a writing project of your own.

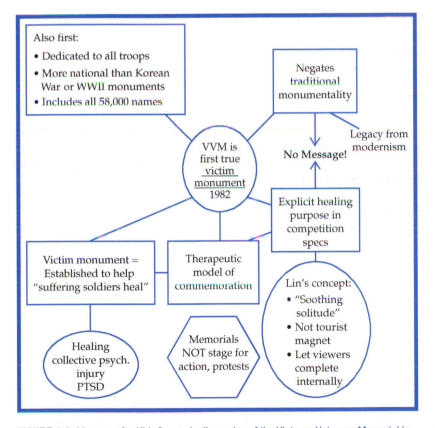

FIGURE 3.6 Idea map for Kirk Savage's discussion of the Vietnam Veterans Memorial in Chapter 6 of *Monument Wars*, reprinted at the end of this chapter

Describing What Verbal Texts Say and Do

Descriptive outlining enables you to extend your understanding of what a text or visual image *says* into how it is working rhetorically (what it *does*).[4] Some people call these *"says/does* outlines." In them, a *says* **statement** summarizes the content of a stretch of text (a sentence, a paragraph, a group of paragraphs), and a *does* **statement** sums up how that particular piece of text functions within the whole. It might *describe* or *explain* or *argue,* for example. For help with conceptualizing what texts can *do*, see the list of Verbs That Describe What Texts Do on the next page.

Does statements should not repeat content but should focus instead on the purpose or function of that content in relation to the overall purpose of the larger text. Here are some sample *does* statements:

- Offers an anecdote to illustrate previous point
- Introduces a new reason for adopting policy
- Provides statistical evidence
- Summarizes the previous section

Using *does* and *says* statements to create a descriptive outline will help you see how a text works at the micro level, paragraph by paragraph, section by section. This kind of analysis is particularly useful as a way to begin a summary as well as to focus an analysis or critique of an author's rhetorical methods.

Sample Does-Says Statements

To illustrate, we offer the following sample *does* and *says* statements for the three opening paragraphs of the Savage selection printed at the end of this chapter. We begin each set with a *does* statement to keep the focus on the function of a given paragraph within the unfolding structure of the larger text. Notice that the implicit subject of the *does* and *says* verbs is the text itself.

Paragraph 1
Does: Announces a new way of understanding Maya Lin's accomplishment with the Vietnam Veterans Memorial (VVM)
Says: VVM is first true victim monument, designed to help soldiers heal

Paragraph 2
Does: Places VVM in context with other war memorials
Says: VVM is "first" in a number of categories

Paragraph 3
Does: Discusses VVM in relation to monument traditions preceding it
Says: VVM is "fundamental" break with tradition because it delivers no message

---

[4]We first learned about descriptive outlining from Kenneth Bruffee's work in *A Short Course in Writing,* 3rd ed. (Boston: Little Brown, 1985), 103. Print.

VERBS THAT DESCRIBE WHAT TEXTS DO

Each of these verbs might be used to complete a phrase such as "this paragraph [or section] _____."

adds (e.g., adds detail)	evaluates	proposes
analyzes	explains	qualifies
argues	expresses	questions
asks	extends	quotes
cites	generalizes	reasons
compares	illustrates	rebuts
connects	informs	reflects
continues	interprets	repeats
contradicts	introduces	states
contrasts	lists	speculates
demonstrates	narrates	suggests
describes	offers	summarizes
details	opposes	supports
dramatizes	predicts	synthesizes
elaborates	presents	traces
	projects	uses

Descriptive outlining will give you analytical distance that will prove to be not only a powerful tool for rhetorical analysis, but also a valuable aid for your own writing. When you are revising, asking yourself what specific sections of your text are doing and saying—and what you want them to do and say—will help you focus on both content and organization as you compose or revise. Even during composing, asking yourself what you want your text to *do* next will often help you figure out what to *say* next.

At first you may find that creating a descriptive outline is more difficult than you expect because it forces a slow rereading of a text's distinct parts. But that slowed-down analysis is the purpose of the technique. It is designed to prompt thought that goes beyond scooping up surface meaning. Rereading this way will take you to a clearer understanding of the argument and structure of the text you are examining. Trust us!

• FOR WRITING AND DISCUSSION

ON YOUR OWN

Make a paragraph-by-paragraph descriptive outline of a book chapter or article that you have been assigned to read in one of your other courses (or of another text as your teacher directs), providing one *does* sentence and one *says* sentence for each paragraph. Then, from the set of *does* and *says* statements, create an idea map that represents visually the relationship or hierarchy of ideas in the article or chapter. For models, use Figure 3.6 and the sample descriptive outline based on the opening paragraphs of the Savage excerpt at the end of this chapter.

WITH YOUR CLASSMATES

Working in small groups, compare your idea maps and descriptive outlines. Each group can then draw revised idea maps and put them on the board or an overhead for discussion. •

Describing What Visual Texts Do

The strategies of descriptive outlining can also help you understand more deeply the role and significance of a text's visual features in relation to its verbal content. Again, such analysis can go beyond deepening your understanding of texts and help with your own writing. How? It will help you articulate what kind of a visual you need for a given project; furthermore, in collaborative situations in both school and the workplace it can help you clarify what to ask someone else—a group or team member—to help you find.

With visual images, we typically reverse the analysis process and start with a *says* statement. (If it helps, you might think of it as a "depicts" or "shows" statement.) You will want this visual *says* statement to present the image on its own terms, describing it as if it stood alone, without the text accompanying it. Make it a literal description of the visual image itself.

For example, consider the image from the Peace Corps Web site that we reproduce in Chapter 4 (p. 85). For now, let's ignore both the overall screen layout and the links on the left and instead focus on what we would need to include in a says-statement description of the photograph and the text box inside it: "Ready to make a difference in 2013?" To capture what we see as we study the image, this says-statement needs to mention the delighted smiles on the faces of the young girl and her mentor/teacher (no doubt a Peace Corps volunteer), the direction of their gazes, and the juxtaposition of this happy scene with the recruiting message in the box on the right.

In contrast, a *does* statement about an image needs to consider its context and purpose. Why is this image there? What work does it do, or lead our eyes to do? A good way to start is to consider the enhancing, supporting, and extending categories we discussed earlier. For Figure 4.3, a good *does* statement might note that the photograph *enhances* the recruiting message by suggesting the volunteer is making a difference in the life of the girl, and by implication, so may "you," the viewer of the site. (The small print answers a presumed "yes" to the "ready?" question by saying: "The Peace Corps has a position for for you," and a link to "Learn more."

The following list provides sample *does-says* statements about two images presented earlier in this chapter: the shocking evidence of the destruction caused by Hurricane Sandy in Figure 3.4, and the more abstract image in Figure 3.5, for which numerous interpretations are possible. Notice again that the subject of the verb in the *does* statement is understood to be the text itself—in these cases, the images.

Figure 3.4

Does: Provides "before-and-after" images that support the validity of the headline's question about the future and document the destruction to which the people quoted in the article are reacting.

Says/Depicts: contrasting scenes of the Funtime Pier show children at play in the sand during the summer and the amusement pier's owner walking among the remnants of destroyed buildings and rides.

For the next example, we combine *says* and *does* statements into one sentence that could be used in a discussion of the combined text and image:

> The drawing by Randy Mack Bishop in Figure 3.5, which depicts three figures headed away from us with their arms around each other and seeming to rise off the ground together as they head away from us, their arms around each other, extends Maureen Dowd's text about organ donation with an inspirational image representing an abstract idea of mutual support.

Writing About How Texts Work: Guidelines and Two Examples

Probably the best way to demonstrate that you have "listened" carefully to a text is to compose a **summary**—a condensed version of a text's main points written in your own words, conveying the author's main ideas but eliminating supporting details. When your goal is to describe not only the content of a text but *how* that text makes its points, a still more powerful technique is to write a **rhetorical précis**.

How Summaries Are Used in Academic and Workplace Settings

Composing a summary requires you to articulate the gist of a text. Summaries take many forms and fulfill a variety of functions in the workplace as well as academic courses. In research papers, you will often present brief summaries of sources to give readers an overview of another writer's perspective or argument, thus bringing another voice into the conversation. If the source is particularly important to your project, you might write a longer summary—perhaps even a full paragraph. The ability to write a good summary will be valuable for any number of academic assignments that ask you to report your understanding of what a text says (see p. 34), particularly for the literature reviews typically required in science classes. Summaries are also likely to be useful in a persuasive "take-a-stand" paper: first, to provide evidence that supports your view, and second, to present fully and accurately any arguments that oppose your view (after which you will try to counter these arguments). Furthermore, for a paper in the social or physical sciences, you will often be expected to write an **abstract** of your own work (a summary), because it is conventional in these fields to begin a published work with a highly condensed overview in case busy readers don't have time to read the whole text. In business and professional life, the equivalent of an abstract is an **executive summary,** a section that appears at the front of any major business report or proposal. Summary writing, in other words, is one of the most frequently used forms of writing that you will encounter in your academic and professional life.

Summaries will vary in length according to purpose. At times, you may summarize a text in one or two sentences as a way of invoking the authority of another voice (probably an expert) to support your points. For example, suppose you wanted to use Savage's concept of the therapeutic model of commemoration to contrast the Vietnam Veteran's Memorial with a statue of a nineteenth-century general mounted on a horse. You might write something like the following:

> Unlike the statue of the general on his horse, which is intended to commemorate the general's heroism, the Vietnam Veterans Memorial (VVM) has what Kirk Savage calls a "therapeutic" purpose. In his book Monument Wars, Savage lays out the advantages of the "therapeutic model of commemoration" that is embodied in Maya Lin's design for the VVM. Elements of this model include a healing purpose, absence of a "message," and an overall setting that will allow viewers to explore the meaning of the monument internally.

After this brief summary introducing the concept, you could go on describe the extent to which the heroic monument you are considering possesses these or contrasting qualities, perhaps calling upon Savage's discussion of hero monuments elsewhere in his book. (Its index has multiple references to the topic.)

At other times, summaries may be one of your main purposes for writing. A typical college assignment might ask you to summarize the arguments of two writers and then analyze the differences in their views. In the summary part of such an assignment, your professor will expect you to demonstrate your understanding of what might be quite complex arguments. The guidelines that follow will help you do so.

Guidelines for Writing a Summary

Writing a fair and accurate summary requires that you (1) identify a text's main ideas, (2) state them in your own words, and (3) omit supporting details. For efficiency and thoroughness, the best first step is to create a descriptive outline of the text you need to summarize, using *does* statements to clarify its structure and *says* statements to put in your own words the main point of each paragraph. (A first draft of your summary could be simply your sequencing of all

> **BOX 3.1 COMPOSING A SUMMARY**
>
> **Step 1:** Read the text first for its main points.
>
> **Step 2:** Reread carefully and make a descriptive outline.
>
> **Step 3:** Write out the text's thesis or main point. (Suppose you had to summarize the whole argument in one sentence.)
>
> **Step 4:** Identify the text's major divisions or chunks. Each division develops one of the stages needed to make the whole main point. Typically, these stages or parts might function as background, review of the conversation, summary of opposing views, or subpoints in support of the thesis.
>
> **Step 5:** Try summarizing each part in one or two sentences.
>
> **Step 6:** Now combine your summaries of the parts into a coherent whole, creating a condensed version of the text's main ideas in your own words.

your *says* statements.) Making a descriptive outline will help you see the text's different sections and organizational strategies. Almost all texts—even very short ones—can be divided into a sequence of sections in which groups of paragraphs chunk together to form distinctive parts of the argument or discussion. Identifying these parts or chunks and how they function within the whole text is particularly helpful because you can write a summary of each chunk, then combine the chunks.

We present a step-by-step process for summary writing in Box 3.1. To illustrate the process, we present a summary written by a student we'll call "Jaime" of the *UC Berkeley Wellness Letter*'s "Chew on This" article (p. 25). Because this article is so brief, it may at first seem that it would be difficult to summarize, but that shortness makes it a good example of the process of omitting details in order to boil a text down to its essence.

Sample Summary with Attributive Tags

In the following summary of "Chew on This," notice that Jaime regularly refers back to the article itself by using what are called "attributive tags" or "signal phrases," such as, "the author reports," "it presents," "the article suggests," and so forth. These phrases serve as signals that Jaime is summarizing someone else's ideas rather than stating his own. Using phrases like these will help you avoid one of the big mistakes that novice writers make when summarizing: making the original author invisible. (For more detailed suggestions about using phrases like these, see Chapter 6, pp. 139–142.)

We invite you to read over Jaime's summary and evaluate it against the checklist in Box 3.2. What might you say or do differently to make this a better summary? Could you make it shorter still, perhaps by just one line, without cutting important information?

BOX 3.2 CHECKLIST FOR EVALUATING SUMMARIES

Good summaries must be fair, accurate, and complete. Use this checklist to evaluate drafts of a summary.

☐ Is the summary economical and precise?

☐ Is the summary neutral in its representation of the original author's ideas, omitting the current writer's own opinions?

☐ Does the summary reflect the proportionate coverage given various points in the original text?

☐ Are the original author's ideas expressed in the summary writer's own words?

☐ Does the summary use attributive tags (also called "signal phrases"), such as "Savage describes," to remind readers whose ideas are being presented?

☐ Does the summary quote sparingly (usually only key ideas or phrases that cannot be said precisely except in the original author's own words)?

☐ Will the summary stand alone as a unified and coherent piece of writing?

☐ Is the original source cited so that readers can locate it?

Jaime's Summary of "Chew on This"

[1]"Chew on This," published as a Last Word feature in the February 2012 *UC Berkeley Wellness Letter*, briefly updates readers about recent research regarding whether gum-chewing is beneficial and suggests that any benefits are minor or do not last for long. [2]The article's unnamed author reports that the most likely benefit of gum chewing is increased saliva flow, which prevents cavities, especially with sugar-free gum containing xylitol. [3]But regular brushing and flossing are more important. [4]The article reports in somewhat more detail about studies published recently in the scholarly journal *Appetite*. [5]Regarding the possibility that gum-chewing helps prevent weight gain, one study found that the main weight-control benefit comes not from burning calories but from chewing gum instead of snacking on something with higher calories. [6]Another study published in *Appetite* focused on the possibility of improved cognitive performance from gum-chewing and reported that recent studies show that the benefits are brief and that not everyone experiences them.

Guidelines for Writing a Rhetorical Précis

A **rhetorical précis** (pronounced *pray-SEE*) provides a structured model for describing the rhetorical strategies of a text, as well as for capturing the gist of its content. It differs from a summary in that it is less neutral, more analytical, and comments directly on the method of the original text. ("Précis" means "concise summary.") Highly structured, it is designed for presentation of insights about a text from the perspective of a rhetorical reader. If you think of a summary as primarily a brief representation of what a text says, then you might think of a rhetorical précis as a brief representation of what a text both says and does. Although less common than a summary, a rhetorical précis is a particularly useful way to sum up your understanding of how a text works rhetorically.

Part summary and part analysis, the rhetorical précis is also a powerful skill-building exercise often assigned as a highly structured four-sentence paragraph (see Box 3.3).[5] As explained in the box, these sentences provide a condensed statement of a text's main point (the summary part), followed by brief statements about its essential rhetorical elements: the methods, purpose, and intended audience (the analytical part). Note the ways in which Jaime's four-sentence rhetorical précis of the *Wellness Letter* article is similar to and different from his six-sentence summary of the article.

Jaime's Rhetorical Précis

[1]A UC Berkeley Wellness Letter article, "Chew on This" (Feb. 2012), summarizes recent research on the possible benefits of gum-chewing and reports that so far, this research shows only small or brief benefits. [2]The author notes first that gum-chewing may increase saliva flow that prevents cavities (but should not replace brushing and flossing), but then takes a "maybe" approach when reporting that gum-chewing's possible benefits for both weight maintenance and brain stimulation are limited and short-lived.

BOX 3.3 HOW TO STRUCTURE A RHETORICAL PRÉCIS

Sentence 1: Name of author, genre, and title of work, date in parentheses; a rhetorically accurate verb (such as *claims*, *argues*, *asserts*, *suggests*); and a "that" clause containing the major assertion or thesis statement in the work

Sentence 2: An explanation of how the author develops and supports the thesis, usually in chronological order

Sentence 3: A statement of the author's apparent purpose

Sentence 4: A description of the intended audience and/or the relationship the author establishes with the audience

---

[5]Our rhetorical précis assignment and illustration are based on the work of Margaret K. Woodworth, "The Rhetorical Précis," *Rhetoric Review* 7 (1988): 156–65. Print.

[3]The fact that this article fills the newsletter's customary spot for brief research reports establishes the author's purpose as informative, but its informal tone suggests that it is written to amuse as well as to inform. [4]The author assumes an audience of well-educated readers who have high interest in health and wellness issues but a cautious attitude toward research findings, and thus is able to use a humorous tone as well as a clever, punning title that implicitly warns that what is being reported is something to "chew on" but not to be taken as certain.

A Brief Writing Project

This assignment asks you to apply what you've learned about reading rhetorically in this chapter by listening carefully to a text and writing about what you "hear." Working with a text identified by your instructor, use the strategies suggested in this chapter to prepare three short assignments, each of which will help you move on to the next.

1. A descriptive outline of the text
2. A 150- to 200-word summary of the text
3. A four-sentence rhetorical précis of the text

Chapter Summary

Building on Chapter 2's recommendations about analyzing the rhetorical contexts of the texts you are reading in relation to your own purposes for writing, this chapter has focused on the nuts and bolts of preparing to read, of "listening" carefully to a text, and of writing to describe a text's content and technique.

- To read effectively, you need to read with pen in hand or a keyboard at the ready, interacting with texts by making annotations as you read.
- Before reading, practice specific preparatory strategies such as recalling background knowledge, using visual features to plan and predict, and spot reading.
- While reading, note organizational signals, and mark unfamiliar terms and references, using marginal comments and queries to identify points of difficulty.
- Read visuals carefully as well, noting how—and how well—they enhance, support, or extend the points contained in the text.
- To deepen your understanding of a text, reread carefully, employing such strategies as idea maps and descriptive outlines.
- To compose accurate descriptive accounts of content and rhetorical strategy, use the systematic guidelines we present for summaries and rhetorical précis.

Kirk Savage

The Conscience of the Nation

Kirk Savage is professor of the History of Art and Architecture at the University of Pittsburgh and active in public discussions about monuments and memorials, including the planned Eisenhower Memorial in Washington, D.C., and the 9-11 Memorial in New York City. *Monument Wars* (2009), from which the following selection has been excerpted, received rave reviews in both the popular and scholarly press and was awarded the 2010 Charles C. Eldredge Prize for Distinguished Scholarship in American Art from the Smithsonian American Art Museum. *Washington Post* commentator Philip Kennicott describes Savage as "a monument optimist."[6] His first book, *Standing Soldiers, Kneeling Slaves: Race, War, and Monument in Nineteenth-Century America*, published by Princeton University Press in 1997, examined the representation of race and slavery in monuments. In his faculty biography Savage describes himself as interested generally in the concepts of "traumatic memory" and "therapeutic memorial," concepts he discusses regarding the VVM, the Oklahoma City National Memorial, and plans for the World Trade Center memorial(s) in an essay in *Terror, Culture, Politics: Rethinking 9/11*, ed. Daniel Sherman and Terry Nardin (2006). His blog can be found on his University of Pittsburgh Web page.

From Chapter 6 of Monument Wars[7]

The VVM [Vietnam Veterans Memorial] was the capital's first true victim monument—a monument that existed not to glorify the nation but to help its suffering soldiers heal. Maya Lin's design has bequeathed to us a therapeutic model of commemoration that has become the new common sense of our era but has also opened up difficult questions that have yet to be resolved, or even considered.

Victim mounment— Key term and definition

Track this concept Use for our presentation!

The VVM was a first in many respects. It was the capital's first comprehensive war memorial, dedicated to all U.S. troops who served in a national war rather than a subset from a particular branch, division, or locality. The memorial was more profoundly national in scope than any of the previous memorials erected to the heroes of the Civil War or the world wars. Even the Tomb of the Unknown Soldier in Arlington Cemetery, which included remains of the dead from World

---

[6]"'Monument Wars' Puts Eisenhower Memorial Controversy in Context." *Washington Post.* Washington Post Co., 18 June 2012. Web. 29 June 2012.
[7]Kirk Savage, *Monument Wars.* (Berkeley, CA: U California P, 2009), 266–70. Print. Note: Our footnotes to this excerpt summarize rather than repeat Savage's footnotes.

War I, World War II, Korea, and Vietnam and served as a national focal point for ritual services on Memorial Day and Veterans Day, did not satisfy the felt need for comprehensive recognition of the nation's servicemen.[8] The VVM was the first—and is still the only—war memorial in the capital and the nation that claims to include the names of all the U.S. dead. Maya Lin's sunken black granite walls were designed, first and foremost, with this intention—to carry the names of the fifty-eight thousand U.S. servicemen who lost their lives in the war. The explicit healing purpose of the monument drove this logic of comprehensiveness. Once born, though, the new type could be adapted to other purposes. The Korean War Veterans Memorial and the World War II memorial are also comprehensive, though quite different in tone and content from Lin's prototype; neither one attempts the reproduction of individual names at the heart of her design.

Note: "explicit healing purpose"

3   Dedicated in 1982, Lin's walls have since become the most talked-about, most written-about monument in American history. The memorial is now so popular a fixture on the Mall that we can forget how radical her proposal once was and how close her critics came to stopping it altogether. Lin herself has called her work an antimonument—a negation of traditional monumentality. She brought into material form an attitude that had long been articulated in modernist circles. The British art historian Herbert Read, writing in the late 1930s in the aftermath of the catastrophes of World War I and the Spanish Civil War, had declared that in the modern world "the only logical monument would be some sort of negative monument." A negative monument, he assumed, would have to be "a monument to disillusion, to despair, to destruction."[9] Lin, however, found a way to break this logic that conflated negation and disillusion. She did not intend her memorial to deliver a message of protest against war (as did Picasso's huge mural *Guernica*, about which Read was writing). The break with tradition was more fundamental: her memorial avoided delivering *any* message. The meaning was to be generated by the viewers themselves, in their experience of the place.

"modernist circles"?

No message in the VVM ++ Import! NOT a protest [Find Guernica online—just curious] ☆

Uh-oh. Not familiar to me! Ask Prof. R. re using this background Look up iconoclasm

4   If this sounds vaguely familiar, that is because the "antimonument" idea tapped into an old American tradition of iconoclasm that long predated modernist ideas of negation. After all, it was in 1800 that John Nicholas had proposed a "blank tablet" for Washington on which "every man could

---

[8]Savage's footnote here notes an author who has also made this point.
[9]Savage inserts a footnote here indicating the sources of both Lin's and Read's remarks.

write what his heart dictated." Like the blank tablet, Lin's simple wall of names awaits completion by individual view- ers and indeed the notes and other memorabilia visitors have left at the wall make manifest that internal process, like the act of writing Nicholas contemplated. On the one hand, Lin's design was a work of high conceptual art totally alien to the veterans who sponsored the monument; on the other, it repre- sented an aspiration toward "living memory" that must have resonated with the antiauthoritarian, democratic impulses of many in their constituency.

Connects to the above

Maybe find article or video about memorabilia— maybe 30-year anniversary

As many have already pointed out, the idea of a nontra- ditional, nondidactic war memorial was not Lin's alone. She submitted a design in response to an open competition, whose program specified that the memorial must list the names of all the American war dead; must avoid political interpretations of the war, pro or con; and must harmonize with its tranquil park setting in the new Constitution Gardens. The memorial's statement of purpose, while affirming that it would "provide a symbol of acknowledgment of the [soldiers'] courage, sac- rifice, and devotion to duty," ended in this way: "The Memo- rial will make no political statement regarding the war or its conduct. It will transcend those issues. The hope is that the creation of the Memorial will begin a healing process."[10] Lin's genius lay in her ability to create a simple and beautiful solu- tion to this novel and difficult program.

5

"nondidactic"?

Healing ex- plicitly in statement of purpose

Note: "Lin's genius"!

Thus the nation's first "therapeutic" memorial was born— a memorial made expressly to heal a collective psychological injury. It is surely no coincidence that the monument cam- paign that led to Lin's selection began at about the time that "posttraumatic stress disorder" entered the official psychiat- ric diagnostic manual.[11] The man who hatched the campaign, Jan Scruggs, was a Vietwtraumatic stress. Scruggs wanted the monument to serve a dual healing function: for the veterans themselves, who had endured not only the trauma of combat but a crushing rejection from society afterward, and for the nation that had been so bitterly divided over the justice of the cause. The last thing he and his fellow veterans in charge of the monument campaign wanted was to reignite the politi- cal conflicts that were still fresh in everyone's mind, in part because they had been so dramatized in protests on the Mall

6

---

[10]Savage's lengthy footnote here cites the source of the quote and refers to other refer- ences to the VVM as "therapeutic" and "healing," including a book published after his was in production.

[11]Savage's footnote here refers readers to discussions about veterans and trauma.

itself. The monument was intended to rally Americans around the simple idea that the veterans of the war needed recognition and support[.]...

7   ... Lin had ... soothing solitude in mind when she designed her entry for the west end of Constitutional Gardens. Her proposal did not envision the memorial as a crowded tourist magnet like the Lincoln Memorial. Whereas that memorial was sited conspicuously on a high platform at the end of the east-west axis [of the Mall], the VVM site was screened by trees, and Lin hid the memorial even further by situating the walls below grade. The approach through Constitution Gardens created a moment of surprise: visitors would happen upon the walls unfolding in front of them, a revelation reminiscent of those [that 19th century landscape designer Andrew Jackson] Downing had had in mind for the Mall.[12]

8   This quiet, secluded experience seemed the opposite of the collective marches and assemblies held out in the open, which had defined the image of the Mall in the period from the civil rights movement to the antiwar struggle. Nevertheless, Lin's design was an outgrowth of that recent history. The experience she wanted to create developed organically from the Mall's twentieth-century psychology with its introspective quality already evident in the Lincoln Memorial and the axis to the Capitol. Lin wanted to turn that introspective experience further inward. "I thought the experience of visiting the memorial," she said later, "should be a private awakening, a private awareness of [individual] loss." For her, memorial spaces were not "stages where you act out, but rather places where something happens within the viewer."[13] Although her emphasis on the subjectivity of viewer response was already inherent in the spatial turn public monuments began to take in the early twentieth century, her understanding of that subjective process as fundamentally private belonged to a more recent cultural turn away from political activism and ritual and toward self-exploration.

---

[12]Savage's footnote here refers readers to another author's discussion of Lin's intentions when she entered the competition.

[13]Savage uses a footnote here to source the quote in comments from Lin at a 1995 symposium.

CHAPTER 4

Questioning a Text

A good question is never answered. It is not a bolt to be tightened into place but a seed to be planted and to bear more seed toward the hope of greening the landscape of idea.

—John Ciardi

Whereas the previous chapter focused on listening to a text *with the grain* in order to understand it as fully as possible, in this chapter we focus on questioning a text, which involves reading it analytically and

In this chapter, you will learn:

A repertoire of useful strategies that will help you question a text, explore your responses to it, and prepare a rhetorical analysis of it. These strategies analyze

- An author's use of the three classical rhetorical appeals identified by Aristotle: *ethos, logos,* and *pathos*
- An author's use of language to create a persona, connect with the audience, and represent ideas as reasonable and compelling
- The ideology or worldview of a text; that is, the set of values and beliefs invoked by it
- The impact of visual elements that may be used to enhance, support, and extend rhetorical appeals

To demonstrate how such strategies can enable you to write critical analyses that will be valued by college professors, the chapter closes with

- Activities for exploring your responses to a text
- Guidelines for writing a rhetorical analysis
- A sample rhetorical analysis paper based on Atul Gawande's op-ed, "A Lifesaving Checklist," reprinted at the end of this chapter (pp. 99–100).

skeptically, *against the grain.* If you think of listening to a text as letting the author take a turn in a conversation, then you might think of questioning the text as your opportunity to respond to the text by interrogating it, raising points of agreement and disagreement, thinking critically about its argument and methods, and then talking back.

What It Means to Question a Text

Learning to question a text is central to your academic success in college. Your professors will ask you to engage with texts in ways that you may not be used to. They expect you to do more than just "bank" the knowledge you glean from reading; they expect you to use this knowledge to do various kinds of intellectual work—to offer your own interpretations or evaluations, to launch a research project of your own, to synthesize ideas from a number of readings, and to draw independent conclusions. Such thoughtful reading of texts begins with your questions addressed to the text and its author. Academics sometimes refer to the questioning process as interrogation of a text, an apt metaphor that likely brings to mind scenes from television shows where police officers or attorneys grill suspects and witnesses (metaphoric stand-ins here for a text that requires examination).

Importantly, questioning does not necessarily mean fault-finding, and it certainly doesn't mean dismissing an author's ideas wholesale. Rather, it entails carefully interrogating a text's claims and evidence and its subtle forms of persuasion so that you can make sound judgments and offer thoughtful responses. Your job in critiquing a text is to be "critical." However, the meanings of the term *critical* include "characterized by careful and exact evaluation and judgment," not simply "disagreement" or "harsh judgment." In questioning a text, you bring your critical faculties to bear on it along with your experience, knowledge, and opinion. But you must do so in a way that treats the author's ideas fairly and makes judgments that can be supported by textual evidence.

The close, even-handed examination of a text's content and persuasive strategies is greatly facilitated by using the three classical rhetorical appeals identified by Aristotle:

* *Ethos:* the persuasive power of the author's credibility or character
* *Logos:* the persuasive power of the author's reasons, evidence, and logic
* *Pathos:* the persuasive power of the author's appeal to the interests, emotions, and imagination of the audience

Although these three appeals interconnect and sometimes overlap—for example, a writer may use a touching anecdote both to establish credibility as an empathetic person (*ethos*) and to play on the reader's emotions (*pathos*)—we introduce them separately to emphasize their distinct functions as means of persuasion.

"I don't just record ideas when I read, I contend with the ideas the book presents; I work with them, engage in combat with them, synthesize them into concepts I already know, and then come up with my own ideas. I engage with the world and develop an original vision. This is the process that writers use."[1]

—Maxine Hong-Kingston

Examining a Writer's Credibility and Appeals to Ethos

To change readers' minds about something, writers must make themselves credible by projecting an image of themselves that will gain their readers' confidence. In most cases, writers want to come across as knowledgeable, fair-minded, and trustworthy. To examine a writer's credibility, ask yourself, "Do I find this author believable and trustworthy? Why or why not?"

Strong academic readers always try to find out as much as possible about an author's background, interests, political leanings, and general worldview. Sometimes they have independent knowledge of the writer, either because the writer is well known or has been discussed in class, or because an article has a headnote or footnote describing the author's credentials. Often, though, readers must discern a writer's personality and views from the text itself by examining content, tone, word choice, figurative language, organization, and other cues that help create an image of the writer in their minds. Explicit questions to ask might include these:

1. Does this writer seem knowledgeable?
2. What does the writer like and dislike?
3. What are this writer's biases and values?
4. What seems to be the writer's mood? (Angry? Questioning? Meditative? Upset? Jovial?)
5. What is the writer's approach to the topic? (Formal or informal? Logical or emotional? Distant and factual, or personal? Mixed in attitude?)
6. What would it be like to spend time in this writer's company?

● FOR WRITING AND DISCUSSION

ON YOUR OWN

1. To help you consider an author's image and credibility, try these activities the next time you are assigned a reading. Describe in words your

---

[1]Maxine Hong-Kingston, in *Speaking of Reading*, ed. Nadine Rosenthal (Portsmouth, NH: Heinemann, 1995), 178. Print.

image of the author as a person (or draw a sketch of this person). Then try to figure out what cues in the text produced this image for you. Finally, consider how this image of the writer leads you to ask more questions about the text. You might ask, for example, "Why is this writer angry? Why does this writer use emotionally laden anecdotes rather than statistics to support his or her case? What is this writer afraid of?"

2. Try these activities with the **op-ed article** by Atul Gawande at the end of this chapter. What kind of an image does he create for himself in this text? How would you describe him in words or portray him in a drawing? Take a few minutes to find and jot down the cues in the text that create this image for you.

WITH YOUR CLASSMATES

Compare your impressions of Gawande with those of your classmates. Do any contradictory impressions come up? That is, do some people in the group interpret the textual cues differently? Some people, for example, might see a comment as "forthright" and "frank" while others might see it as "antagonistic" or "hyperbolic." What aspects of his character (as represented in the text) do you as a group agree on? What aspects do you disagree about?   ●

Examining a Writer's Appeals to Reason or Logos

Perhaps the most direct way that writers try to persuade readers is through logic or reason. To convince readers that their perspective is reasonable, skilled writers work to anticipate what their intended readers already believe and then use those beliefs as a bridge to the writer's way of thinking. These writers seek to support their claims through a combination of reasons and evidence.

For example, imagine a writer arguing for stricter gun control laws. This writer wants to root his argument in a belief or value that he and his readers already share, so he focuses on concerns for the safety of schoolchildren. The line of reasoning might go something like this: Because the easy availability of guns makes children no longer safe at school, we must pass strict gun control

EXPLANATION OF OP-ED ARTICLES

Gawande was writing as a guest columnist for the *New York Times*. Such articles are called **"op-eds,"** or "op-ed articles," referring to newspapers' traditional placement of signed opinion columns on the page opposite the editorial page, which presents unsigned editorials approved by an editorial board, editorial cartoons, and letters to the editor.

laws to limit access to guns. Of course, readers may or may not go along with this argument. Some readers, although they share the writer's concern for the safety of schoolchildren, might disagree at several points with the writer's logic: Is the availability of guns the main cause of gun violence at schools or are there other, more compelling causes? Will stricter gun control laws really limit the availability of guns? If this same writer wished to use evidence to strengthen this argument, he might use statistics showing a correlation between the rise in the availability of guns and the rise in gun violence in schools. Here, the writer would be operating on the assumption that readers believe in facts and can be persuaded by these statistics that increased gun violence in schools is linked to the availability of firearms.

Experienced readers are alert to the logical strategies used by authors, and they have learned not to take what may appear as a "reasonable" argument at face value. In other words, they have learned to question or test this reasoning before assenting to the position the author wants them to take. To examine a writer's reasoning, you need to be able to identify and examine carefully the basic elements of an argument—claims, reasons, evidence, and assumptions. The following questions will help you examine a writer's reasoning:

1. What perspective or position does the writer want me to take toward the topic?
2. Do the writer's claims, reasons, and evidence convince me to take this perspective or position?
3. Do I share the assumptions, stated or unstated, that authorize the writer's reasoning and connect the evidence to the claim?

Claims

The key points that a writer wants readers to accept are referred to as **claims**. For example, Kirk Savage's initial claim in the selection at the end of Chapter 3 is that the Vietnam Veterans Memorial was Washington, D.C.'s "first true victim's monument," a term that he immediately defines as "a monument that existed not to glorify the nation but to help its suffering soldiers heal." Or take another example: In the reading at the end of this chapter, Atul Gawande begins his fourth paragraph by calling a decision of the federal Office for Human Research Protections "bizarre and dangerous." Both of these assertions seem contestable, so readers are smart to raise questions, especially about the wording and scope. Is the meaning of key words in the claims clear? Can particular words be interpreted in more than one way? Is the claim overstated? One might ask of Gawande, "Bizarre? How so?" "Dangerous? In what way?" Likewise, one might ask Savage why he does not consider earlier monuments, such as the Tomb of the Unknown Soldier, to be victim monuments.

Reasons

To support a main claim, writers must provide **reasons**. A reason can usually be linked to a claim with the subordinate conjunction "because." Consider the gun control argument mentioned earlier, which we can now restate as a claim with a reason: "We must pass gun control laws that limit access to guns [claim] because doing so will make children safer at school [reason]." This argument has initial appeal because it ties into the audience's likely belief that it is good to make children safe at school. However, as we discussed earlier, the causal links in the argument are open to question. Thus, we see that the "reason" that "doing so will make children safer at school" is a subclaim that itself needs to be supported with reasons and evidence.

Once you've identified the reasons that an author offers for various claims, then you can proceed to examine the adequacy of these reasons. Do they really support the claim? Is the assertion in the reason in need of further support and argument? Do the reasons tie into values, assumptions, and beliefs that the audience shares?

Evidence

The facts, examples, statistics, personal experience, and expert testimony that an author offers to support his or her view of the topic are referred to as **evidence**. To examine an author's use of evidence, consider whether the supporting material is reliable, timely, and adequate to make the case. Ask also whether there is more than one way the evidence can be interpreted.

For example, Gawande is quite convincing as he recounts what he calls the government's "blinkered" reasoning, arguing that although the reasoning may be logical, it is shortsighted. But he does not offer direct statements from the officials with whom he disagrees so that readers can judge for themselves whether the reasoning is "blinkered" or led to a "bizarre" decision. Readers skeptical of his argument might question his rendition of the rationale behind the government ruling. Similarly, in our gun control example, skeptics could question whether the statistical correlation between rising availability of guns and rising gun violence in schools is in fact a causal relationship. The fact that A and B happened at the same time does not mean that A caused B.

Assumptions

In an argument, the often unstated values or beliefs that the writer expects readers to accept without question are referred to as **assumptions**. You can interrogate an argument by questioning, even casting doubt upon, those assumptions. For example, in paragraphs 5 and 6 of his op-ed, Gawande attacks the assumptions underlying the Office for Human Research 's reasoning that the checklist for inserting IV lines and the use of an experimental drug are comparable interventions in medical care. Similarly, part of the hypothetical gun control argument presented earlier is based on an assumption that the proposed legislation will in fact limit the availability of guns. You can question this assumption by pointing to the existence of black markets.

• FOR WRITING AND DISCUSSION

ON YOUR OWN

Find a newspaper or magazine opinion piece (an editorial or an individual opinion piece) and identify its claims, reasons, evidence, and assumptions. You may find that some of these elements are missing or only implied. Then analyze the writer's reasoning in the piece by answering the three questions we listed on page 73 as fundamental to examining a writer's reasoning.

WITH YOUR CLASSMATES

1. Briefly summarize the opinion piece you found and explain your analysis of it to a small group of classmates.
2. After each group member has presented his or her editorial, discuss which group member's editorial involves the most persuasive reasoning and why. Try to focus on the writer's reasoning rather than your own opinions about the matter. Present the results of your group discussion to the rest of the class. If there is disagreement about which piece uses the best reasoning, present more than one to the class and explain the differences in your evaluation. •

Examining a Writer's Strategies for Engaging Readers, or Pathos

The third of the classical rhetorical appeals is to an audience's interests and emotions—the process of engaging readers. How does a writer hook and keep your interest? How does a writer make you care about the subject? How does a writer tweak your emotions or connect an argument with ideas or beliefs that you value?

Rhetoricians have identified four basic ways that writers engage readers at an emotional or imaginative level—by influencing the reader to identify (1) with the writer; (2) with the topic or issue, including people mentioned in the text; (3) with a certain group of fellow readers; or (4) with particular interests, values, beliefs, and emotions. Let's look at each in turn.

In the first approach, writers wanting readers to identify with them might use an informal conversational tone to make a reader feel like the writer's buddy. Writers wanting to inspire respect and admiration might adopt a formal scholarly tone, choose intellectual words, or avoid "I" altogether by using the passive voice—"it was discovered that… ." In the second approach, writers wanting readers to identify with the topic or issue might explain the importance of the issue or try to engage readers' emotions. In urging community action against homelessness, for example, an author might present a wrenching anecdote about a homeless child. Other methods might be the use of vivid details, striking facts, emotion-laden terms and examples, or analogies that explain the unfamiliar in terms of the familiar. In the third approach, writers try to get readers to identify with a certain in-group of people—fellow environmentalists or feminists or Republicans or even fellow intellectuals. Some writers seek to engage readers by creating a role for the reader to play in the text. For example, the author of "Chew on This" puts readers in the role of wondering if there are benefits to chewing gum, and Savage invites readers to consider the appeal of Maya Lin's "antimonument" concept to Vietnam veterans' experiences of alienation from American society. In the fourth approach, writers appeal to readers' interests by getting them to identify with certain values and beliefs. For example, a politician arguing for radical Social Security reform might appeal to young voters' belief that there will be no Social Security available to them when they retire. Awareness of how all of these appeals work will enable you to distance yourself from arguments sufficiently to examine them critically.

● **FOR WRITING AND DISCUSSION**

Examine in detail the ways in which Gawande works to engage readers in his opinion piece at the end of this chapter. On what basis do his opening sentences engage your attention? What kind of a relationship does he try to establish with readers? How does he try to make you care about his topic? What interests and values does he assume his audience shares? Do you consider yourself part of his intended audience? Why or why not? ●

Examining a Writer's Language

Besides looking at a text's classical appeals, you can examine it rhetorically by paying careful attention to its language and style. **Diction,** an umbrella term referring to speakers' and writers' selection and expression of words (including matters of tone and formality), is an important rhetorical tool. So, too, are figurative language, sentence structure and length, and even punctuation. All are techniques through which a writer tries to influence the reader's view of a subject. Consider, for example, the connotation of words. It makes a difference whether a writer calls a person "decisive" rather than "bossy," or an act "bold" rather than "rash." Words like "decisive" and "rash" are not facts; rather, they present the writer's interpretation of behavior. You can question a text by recognizing how the writer makes interpretive words seem like facts.

At times, you might overlook features of the writer's language because they seem natural rather than chosen. You probably seldom stop to think about the significance of, say, the use of italics or a series of short sentences or a particular metaphor. Readers rarely ask what's gained or lost by a writer saying something one way rather than another—for example, calling clear-cut logging in the Northwest a "rape" rather than a "timber extraction process."

Consider, for example, the care that Savage takes to define the concepts of a "victim monument" (par. 1) and "therapeutic monument" (par. 6), as he carefully moves to differentiating the Vietnam Veterans Memorial from other, relatively recent, war memorials in the nation's capital. These definitions provide a necessary foundation to his claim in the Chapter 3 selection's final paragraph that the privacy and subjectivity of experiencing the monument are connected to a cultural turn toward self-exploration. With subject matter so sensitive and emotionally laden with controversy, his prose must move slowly, gently to this abstract point.

For contrast, consider the lighthearted use of language in "Chew on This" (Figure 2.3, p. 25), from the title's almost jokey comparison of literal chewing and thinking to its author's explicit attempt at humor at the end of the article about the limited findings in the cognitive research: "In other words, some people can't think (or walk) and chew gum at the same time." Relaxed language is also evident in the title of the *Appetite* research study that the newsletter has been summarizing: "Cognitive Advantages of Chewing Gum. Now You See Them, Now You Don't" (Figure 2.2, p. 24). Both titles seem to be acknowledging that the research being reported, although seriously undertaken, does not have dire consequences.

However, humorous language can be used with other intentions. Consider the attitude conveyed by Gawande's description of Michigan doctors' behaviors when they followed the checklist he advocates: "they actually wash their hands" (par. 2). Because doctors' hand-washing is something generally assumed to be standard operating procedure, Gawande's insertion of the adverb "actually" not only is likely to catch attention but also to convey an ironic jab of sarcasm. More explicitly sarcastic, but on a far less serious subject, is Garry Trudeau's skewering of the language at high-end coffee shops, shown in Figure 4.1 (p. 78). Here, verbal language and cartooned body language combine to critique the product labeling.

Experienced academic readers develop antennae for recognizing uses of language—some subtle, some less so—to manipulate responses. One way to develop this sensitivity is to ask why a writer makes certain choices rather than others. To what extent do particular word choices suggest calm, reasoned logic, or, conversely, stir emotions? Do the writer's word choices establish her or him as someone on "our" side? Or, if not, on whose side? How does the author establish "our" side? There will always be other ways to say X or Y. As a rhetorical reader, you need to be alert to how a writer's sentences emphasize certain points over others and how word choices may shape your view of the topic at hand. In other words, it is important to consider how the language itself seems designed to win your agreement with that writer's views.

• FOR WRITING AND DISCUSSION

ON YOUR OWN

Returning to the opinion article that you worked with to analyze assumptions for the exercise on page 75 (or another article as your instructor directs), find two or three striking instances of diction (defined on p. 76) that

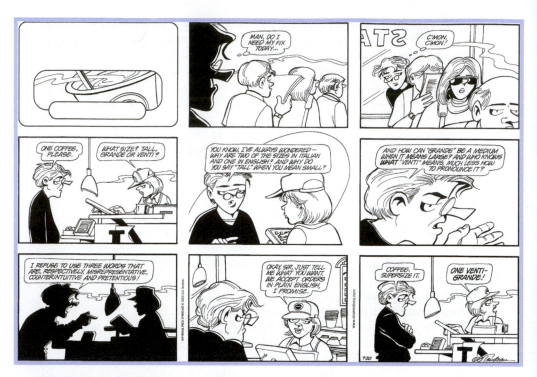

FIGURE 4.1 Doonesbury

call up specific responses in you in terms of the *language* used. Perhaps you can find interpretive words asserted as facts, or adjectives that seem more intense in attitude than what a neutral author would use. How could these sentences be rephrased to convey a different attitude toward the subject matter?

WITH YOUR CLASSMATES

Share and compare your analyses. See if you can reach consensus on the ways that the various writers use special language features for persuasive intent.   •

Examining a Text's Ideology

Another approach to questioning a text is to identify its **ideology**, a technical term for the notion of a worldview. An ideology is a belief system—a coherent set of values and concepts through which we interpret the world. We sometimes think that ideology applies only to other people's worldviews, perhaps those of zealots blinded by a certain rigid set of beliefs. In fact, the term *ideology* applies to all of us. Each of us has our own beliefs, values, and particular ways of looking at the world. Our perspectives are inevitably shaped by family background, religion, personal experience, race, class, gender, sexual orientation, and so on. As you continue with your education, you may even discover that your perspective is influenced by the types of courses you are taking—science majors are sometimes skeptical about the ambiguities of literary texts, for example, and humanities students can similarly resist the details required in laboratory reports. Moreover, each of us is to some extent "blinded" by our worldview, by our own way of seeing. For instance, middle-class persons in the United States, by and large, share a variety of common beliefs: "Hard work leads to success." "Owning your own home is an important good." "Punctuality, cleanliness, and respect for the privacy of others are important values." "All persons are created equal." If we are among the privileged in this country, we literally may not be able to see the existing inequities and barriers to success faced by less privileged Americans.

Yet, to become astute readers, we must look for signals that reveal the ideology informing a text. One way to begin doing so is to look for patterns of opposites or contrasts in a text (sometimes called "binaries") and see which of the opposing terms the writer values more. We generally understand things through contrast with their opposites. We would have no concept of the term *masculine,* for example, without the contrasting term *feminine.* To understand *light,* we have to understand *dark* (or *heavy*). Our concept of *liberal* depends on its contrast with *conservative.* We could list hundreds of these opposites or binaries: civilized is that which is not primitive; free is that which is not enslaved; abnormal is that which is not normal; people of color are those who are not Caucasian. When binaries occur as patterns in a text, one term is generally valued above the other. When you examine the pattern of those values, you can begin to uncover the text's ideology. Sometimes the opposite or devalued terms are only implied, not even appearing in the text. Their absence helps mark the text's ideology.

It is not always immediately evident which terms are valued by a text and which ones are devalued. In such cases, you can often identify a major contrast or binary elsewhere in the text—for example, loggers versus tree huggers, school vouchers versus neighborhood schools, old ways versus new ways, traditional Western medicine versus alternative medicine. You can then determine which of the opposed terms is more valued. Once you can identify the controlling binary, you can often line up other opposites or contrasts appropriately.

If you were to use these oppositions to draw conclusions about the ideology informing Savage's text (see Table 4.1 on page 80), you might say something like the following: "Savage's text gradually builds a case for valuing monuments that honor all soldiers rather than a particular war hero, and that invite subjective interpretations rather than a single, prescribed message. He seems to value the collective sacrifices of war above the traditional emphasis on individual heroes."

TABLE 4.1 • BINARY PATTERNS IN THE SAVAGE EXCERPT IN CHAPTER 3	
Words, Concepts, and Ideas Valued by This Text	**Words, Concepts, and Ideas Not Valued by This Text**
Vietnam Veterans Memorial	Heroes monuments
Victim monument, therapeutic monument	Traditional monuments
Monument as transcending political issues	Political statements on monuments
Tranquil setting for reflection	Monument as setting for protest
Private self-exploration	Activism and ritual

• FOR WRITING AND DISCUSSION

ON YOUR OWN

Return again to the opinion piece in which you analyzed assumptions and language, this time to make a two-column chart of the binaries you find in that text. Put the words, concepts, or ideas that the author values in the left column. Place the opposing words, concepts, or ideas that the author doesn't value in the right column. (Remember, the nonvalued terms may only be implied; they may not actually appear in the text.) Then write a short analysis of the author's ideology, following the model we provided based on Savage's text.

WITH YOUR CLASSMATES

Share your list of binaries with the classmates with whom you have been analyzing editorials. It will be interesting to discover for which texts tracking binaries proved more and less easy or difficult. Again, try to reach consensus to explain these differences. •

Examining a Text's Use of Visual Elements

Images, like words, are often selected and constructed to create particular emotional responses. Photographs, drawings, information graphs, and other images that accompany a text are typically added by the editor of the publication, electronic or print, where the text appears. Nonetheless, these images are another vehicle for rhetorical appeals and thus merit close attention when you analyze any text. The common belief that pictures are more truthful and compelling than words is often true: Visual images are often powerfully persuasive devices. Moreover, images can shape perceptions, emotions, and values without a reader's conscious awareness, thus making their influence particularly seductive.

Questioning the ways in which visual elements make a text more persuasive allows you to step back and avoid the automatic consent implied in the cliché that "seeing is believing."

In Chapter 3, we discussed how consideration of a text's visual elements can help you understand a text's message more fully. We turn now to examining how analysis of these visual elements can help you recognize and question the rhetorical effects of the images themselves. To analyze the ways in which visual elements interact with a textual message, you need to "listen" to the image (what it says or depicts), determine its function (what it does), and analyze the types of appeals it is making (*ethos, logos, pathos*). As we have seen before, these categories may, of course, overlap. We suggest that you begin your analysis of visual elements with the following general questions:

1. How does the visual element relate to the writer's overall point or argument? Is this relationship explicit or implied?
2. How important is this visual element to the author's argument?
3. What kinds of rhetorical appeals does the visual element employ? How does it work rhetorically to influence the intended audience?

Visual Elements and Ethical Appeals

Visual elements frequently enhance a writer's credibility and authority. Thus, an article by a yoga teacher might include a picture of him in an advanced yoga position; an alumni magazine's article about a scientist who has made a scientific breakthrough might include a picture of the scientist working in her lab. Similarly, newspapers and magazines include head shots of syndicated columnists whom they regularly publish. These usually flattering photographs typically offer an image of the writer as smiling and approachable or, perhaps, as intellectual, sophisticated, or down to earth. Head shots also offer information about the author's age, ethnicity, and gender (if not evident from the writer's name), information that is likely to affect our reading of the text, sometimes without our being aware of it. When the subject is affirmative action or racial profiling, for example, the race and perhaps gender of the author are likely to affect readers' perceptions of his or her credibility on the issue.

Of course, these photographs can be misleading. Many writers use the same picture for years, thus preserving the image and credibility of a younger person. The late Ann Landers's column still pictured her as a woman in her mid-forties when she was well into her seventies. Consider the difference it would have made if readers pictured the advice she offered as coming from an elderly, white-haired woman. In short, rhetorical readers need to question even these apparently straightforward visual appeals based on a writer's *ethos* as part of considering their implications. For example, the yoga teacher pictured in an advanced pose may be an expert practitioner of yoga, but does it follow logically, as the picture (and article) implies, that he is a good teacher of yoga?

The key questions to ask in analyzing how visual elements establish a writer's *ethos* are the following:

1. How does the visual element contribute to the writer's image, credibility, and/or authority?
2. How does the image of the author created by the visual element influence your reading of the text?
3. To what extent does the visual image fit the image created by the text?

Visual Elements and Logical Appeals

Drawing on the idea that "seeing is believing," writers often support their claims with visual evidence. Thus, the most common use of visual elements as logical appeals is to supply evidence to verify or support a writer's argument. Whether the visual element is a pie chart, a table of data, or a picture, these elements appear to add concreteness and factuality to an author's claims. Indeed, the genre conventions of scholarly journals dictate that authors provide information graphics to help readers understand and evaluate the strength of the research. Graphics of all sorts are, of course, very important on the Web, where readers with a wide range of literacy skills and experience may access material. Consider, for example, the graphic in Figure 4.2, from TheMint.org, a Web site designed to educate children about financial literacy. It works by using a familiar shape to illustrate an unfamiliar concept. The triangular outline of a pyramid is likely to be recognized across age groups and education levels as a means of contrasting the desirability of goods and behaviors with their advisability, usefulness, or cost. Here, the shape is used to illustrate the financial world's concept of "risk and rewards," contrasting safer, more solid investments at the base with the more risky, but potentially higher-yielding investments at the top.

Visual illustrations are a staple of educational materials, especially for beginners who are new to various subjects and tasks, and they naturally play a central role in academic and journalistic writing that analyzes and critiques the use and quality of the images themselves. In our increasingly visual culture, it is important to question whether images themselves are reliable. The fact is, technology makes it easy for almost anyone to doctor a photo. Consider, for example, the difficulty of solving the popular puzzles in print magazines and newspapers (and on the Web) that invite readers to see how many differences they can find in two seemingly identical photographs. Furthermore, even ordinary photographs can be misleading when they omit the larger context or are published or posted without information about who took the picture or why. Intentional distortion is yet another concern. In the summer of 2006, altered photographs of war-torn Lebanon that a freelancer sold to Reuters caused something of a sensation, less because of the photos' content than because of how readily the news service had been duped. Reuters suspended the

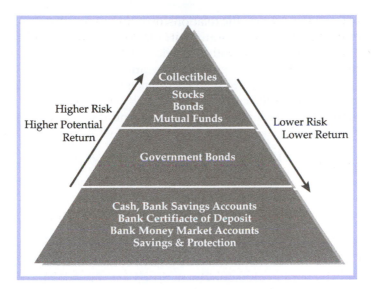

FIGURE 4.2 "Risk and Rewards" graphic from TheMint.org. As the text accompanying the diagram explains, "Investments with lower risks and lower returns are at the bottom of the pyramid—where the large base makes it stable." The Web site notes that investing for a higher return at the top of the pyramid is tempting, but "there is no guarantee that higher-risk investments will actually give you higher returns."

photographer, retracted the photos, and issued an apology.[2] Shortly afterward, the online magazine *Slate* published a critique of news photography in general under the headline "Don't Believe What You See in the Papers," in which writer Jim Lewis points to multiple examples of doctored and misleading photographs. His conclusion offers good advice for rhetorical readers: "Realism is a special effect like any other, and the sooner we realize as much, the better off we'll be . . . . Someday we will approach each photograph we look at with the condign [appropriate] skepticism we bring to each story we read."[3]

The following questions will help you analyze how visuals interact with logical appeals:

1. Does the writer make explicit the relationship between the visual element and his or her argument? If not, chances are good that the visual element was added by an editor who may have interests other than documenting the writer's claims, probably a matter of attracting readership.

---

[2]One photo doubled the amount of smoke rising over Beirut after an Israeli attack; another increased the number of flares dropping from an Israeli plane from one to three and mislabeled them as missiles. See Donald R. Winslow, "Reuters Apologizes over Altered Lebanon War Photos; Suspends Photographer," National Press Photographers Association, 7 Aug. 2006. Web. 27 Mar. 2009.

[3]*Slate*, 10 Aug. 2006. Web. 27 Mar. 2009.

2. How would you define the relationship between the visual and the text? Is it the focal point of the argument? Or does it provide additional support or evidence for the author's claims? Does it seem added primarily as decoration, perhaps to gain readers' attention?
3. Is the visual element providing evidence that is reliable, timely, and adequate to make the case?
4. Does the visual itself make an argument, and if so, is it convincing?

Visual Elements and Audience Appeals

Probably the most powerful rhetorical use of visual elements is to appeal to an audience's emotions, values, and interests—to *pathos*. Three common and often overlapping ways in which visual elements create audience appeals are by setting a tone, fostering identification between reader and content, and evoking emotions and values.

To see how graphic elements can set a tone or context that frames a reader's response, consider your expectations of an article accompanied by an image of Dr. Martin Luther King Jr., delivering his "I Have a Dream" speech in front of the Lincoln Memorial. It seems likely that you would anticipate that the article deals with a serious issue, perhaps civil rights, racial justice, or the role of social protest movements. Similarly, the drawing of the three embracing figures discussed in Chapter 3 (Figure 3.5, p. 53) combined with the headline "Scarred for Life: Courage Begets Courage" may prepare readers for an inspirational article—although, interestingly, neither the drawing nor the headline gives any hint of the specific content of Maureen Dowd's column about organ donation. To discover the meaning of this rather ambiguous image and decidedly dramatic title, readers had to stop their perusal of the newspaper to read the article. Undoubtedly, you can think of many occasions when a striking image caught your attention and triggered an emotional reaction that, in turn, prompted you to read something (or click on a link) that you might otherwise have ignored. Because photographs and drawings are frequently the first thing we notice about a text, it is important to pause both before and after reading to consider how they frame your attitude toward the subject matter.

Visual elements can also create identification with a person, situation, or topic. As we noted in Chapter 3, the smiling faces in the photograph from the Peace Corps Web site in Figure 4.3 convey an enthusiasm that, in context, invites viewers to consider how they might "make a difference" in what was then the year ahead. Even though neither person in the photograph is looking at the camera (or by implication, at us), the contagious quality of their smiles appeals to *pathos* by promoting identification, drawing viewers into the scene. The young girl's body language and facial expression communicate such delight regarding the task that engages her (with pen in her hand), and her teacher looks so pleased, that it is easy to start thinking about how to "make a difference" like the one the blond woman (by implication a Peace Corps volunteer) evidently is making. The accompanying digital text then makes it easy to click and "learn more" about how to make a difference. The clickable phrases

FIGURE 4.3 Screen capture from Peace Corps home page

in the list to the left of the photograph make it still easier to follow up. The links themselves tell potential volunteers exactly what to do—"learn," "connect," "start," and so forth.

As the smiles in Figure 4.3 suggest, closely tied to identification are the emotions and values elicited by visual images. News stories about natural disasters, for example, are frequently accompanied by photographs of distressed children, as are the Web sites of international aid agencies. These images prompt us not only to identify more readily with the human toll but also to feel sadness and compassion, and these emotional responses in turn shape our reading of the news or appeals for funds. Recall the power of the now iconic photograph of the soot-covered New York City firefighters raising the American flag in the aftermath of the 9/11 terrorist attacks, evoking admiration and gratitude for their bravery as well as a sense of patriotic pride. The use of this image, even on a postage stamp, automatically associates whatever text it accompanies with these emotions and values. No matter how compelling the image, however, we still need to ask for what purpose our emotions and values are being evoked. Is the topic at hand really analogous to the heroism of the firefighters on 9/11? Although we cannot avoid "gut" responses to visual images, it is important to stop to consider their intended effect and to question their appropriateness.

The key questions to ask in relation to the use of visuals that appeal to emotions, interests, and values are the following:

1. What purpose does the visual element seem to serve in relation to the text?
2. To which emotions, interests, and values does the visual element appeal? What assumptions are being made about readers' values, interests, and emotions?
3. How do specific parts of the visual element work to elicit a response? How do the parts work together as a whole?
4. Are there other ways of reading or interpreting these elements?

Visual Arguments

The juxtaposition of visual images with verbal text has been a key element in our discussion of visual elements so far. As we have pointed out, rhetorical readers must be alert to the designs that the composers of these texts may have on their audience's thinking. We must examine carefully the claims and assumptions that are implicit within the images as well as perhaps implied in the connections between images and text. We turn now to **visual arguments**, which are combinations of image, text, and layout in which the forwarding of a claim with reasons depends primarily upon the image, even when it is accompanied by verbal text.

First, let's look back at the visual arguments in Figures 1.2 and 1.3 (pp. 13–14), which accompanied our discussion in Chapter 1 of Jack's paper about corn ethanol. This billboard and editorial cartoon typify the way that an image dominates in a visual argument. Words serve to guide readers' quick "reading" of the case being made. However, the underlying structure of the argument—reasons, evidence, assumptions, perhaps even the claim itself—is left for readers to interpret and infer. These two visual arguments focus on a desired or undesired outcome of a chain of causal events entirely implied. Both make an appeal to *pathos* based on assumptions about an audience's emotions and values, and may be successful at invoking in readers the intended positive or negative response, at least initially. Nonetheless, it is very important for a rhetorical reader to pause to take apart not only the explicit claims in such images but the network of implied causes and effects, goods and ills that may or may not factually and logically support those claims. After all, cartoons and billboards are excellent ways to highlight a cause in the interest of building support, but as an academic reader, your interest should be in understanding the complexities behind claims that rely on condensed and implied reasoning.

An audience's willingness and ability to fill in reasons and assumptions to complete a claim is particularly evident in the visual arguments presented in Figures 4.4 and 4.5. These print advertisements are part of the Canadian paper company Domtar's "Paper because" campaign, which is designed to assert paper's value for various business and personal uses. (The campaign extends to videos as well, many of them mocking efforts to "go paperless"). Interestingly, in these advertisements, the actual product being championed is present only by implication. Depending on where the advertisements are placed, the targeted readers might be individual consumers or decision-makers at large corporations. Regardless of their roles, all are invited to fill in the blank ("I should choose paper for _____*what?*_____") at the same time that they mentally fill in the reason for doing so ("because…_____*why?*_____"). The small print in each ad prompts a line of reasoning, one connecting to a place where many consumers literally touch paper in their everyday lives, the other promoting the company's commitment to the environment.

The For Writing and Discussion activity that follows invites you to fill in the blanks of these visual arguments by imagining yourself in a decision-making process about whether to use paper for something, as an individual, a family, a student group, or a business. As you attempt to compose an argument leading

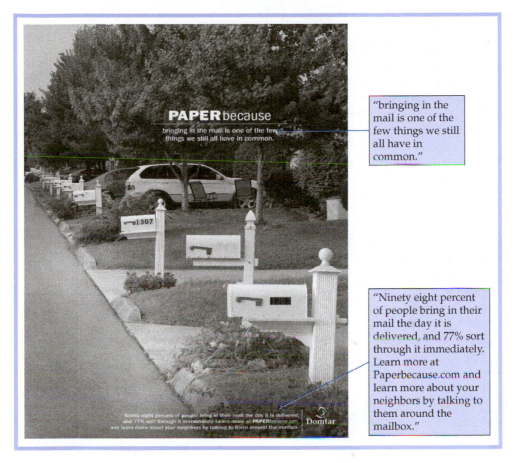

FIGURE 4.4 Advertisement advocating the value of paper products, from Domtar, a major North American paper and pulp company.

in one direction or the other, consider what reasoning Domtar's advertising strategies invite. What assumptions do the strategies seem to call for? Are they assumptions that you accept, or do they need to be argued? Overall, does the implied chain of reasoning lead you to choose paper? Why or why not?

● FOR WRITING AND DISCUSSION

ON YOUR OWN

Try translating one of the visual arguments in this chapter or in Chapter 1 into a paragraph-long written argument. To do so, you will need to identify the central claims made by the figure's combination of verbal and visual elements, the evidence used (or implied) in support of those claims, and the assumptions that connect the claims and evidence.

FIGURE 4.5 Advertisement advocating the value of paper products, from Domtar, a major North American paper and pulp company.

WITH YOUR CLASSMATES

Share your written version of the visual argument with a group of classmates and together apply the questioning strategies suggested throughout this chapter to analyze and assess the argument's persuasiveness. •

Exploring Your Responses to a Text

In this section, instead of suggesting questioning strategies, we explain approaches to interrogating a text that ask you simply to explore your own reactions to it. These approaches encourage you to record your first reactions to a text and then, after reflection, your more sustained and considered responses.

Before/After Reflections

To consider how much a text has influenced your thinking, try writing out some before and after reflections by freewriting your responses to the following statements. These questions hearken back to the questions for rhetorical reading we posed in Chapter 1 (pp. 10–11), where we suggested that before reading a text, you should consider what its author seems to assume readers think about the subject at hand and how that author works to change such thinking by the time you finish reading. To illustrate, after the following list of before/after questions, we provide Abby's responses to the first two questions in connection with the Gawande article.

1. What effect is this text trying to have on me? What kind of change does the writer hope to make in my view of the subject?
2. Before reading this text, I believed this about the topic: _____ _____. But after reading the text, my view has changed in these ways: _____.
3. Although the text has persuaded me that_____ _____, I still have the following doubts:_____.
4. The most significant questions this text raises for me are these: _____ _____.
5. The most important insights I have gotten from reading this text are these: _____.

Abby's Initial Before/After Reflections About Gawande's Argument
Concerning Medical Checklists

1. Gawande wants his readers to be aware of a serious problem with medical procedures. I don't think I'm part of the primary intended audience, which is probably medical doctors and members of Congress, but I am certainly someone who could send emails to Washington to ask about this—an action that his last sentence calls for by implication.

2. Before reading this text, I knew nothing about the issue, and certainly assumed that doctors always wash their hands. But now I am worried!

The Believing and Doubting Game

Playing the believing and doubting game with a text is a powerful strategy both for recording your reactions to it and for stimulating further thinking. Developed by writing theorist Peter Elbow, the believing and doubting game will stretch your thinking in surprising ways. Elbow called it a "game" because its purpose is not to commit to ideas, but to try them out. Begin on the positive side by freewriting all the reasons why you believe the writer's argument. Then freewrite all the reasons why you doubt the same argument. In the "believe" portion, try to look at the world through the text's perspective, adopting its ideology, actively supporting its ideas and values. Search your mind for any life experiences or memories of reading and research that help you sympathize with and support the author's point of view or ideas. If you find the author's ideas upsetting, dangerous, or threatening, the believing game may challenge—even disturb—you. It takes courage to try to believe views that you feel are dead wrong or contrary to your most deeply held beliefs. Nevertheless, to be a strong rhetorical reader, you need to look at the world through perspectives different from your own.

According to Elbow, the believing game helps you grow intellectually by letting you take in new and challenging ideas. In contrast, the doubting game helps you solidify your present identity by protecting you from outside ideas. Like an antiballistic missile, the doubting game lets you shoot down ideas that you don't like. The "doubt" portion of this game thus reverses the believing process. Here, you try to think of all of the problems, limitations, or weaknesses in the author's argument. You brainstorm for personal experiences or memories that refute or call into question the author's view. Of course, in turn, the doubting game can be unsettling if you already agree with the author's views because it asks you to articulate arguments that take a stand against your own beliefs.

In the following example, Abby works on developing ideas for her rhetorical analysis of the Gawande op-ed by playing the believing and doubting game. She followed her writing instructor's advice to write rapidly, using bullet points as needed to speed things up. She allowed herself no more than ten minutes each for believing and doubting. (She set the timer on her cell phone.) Note how this exercise promotes critical thinking that goes beyond just expressing subjective opinions. The results of playing the believing and doubting game are nearly always a bit surprising.

Abby's Believing-Doubting Game Freewrite

Believe Wow. This guy's claims scare me to death. How could a bureaucracy make something this good stop? He seems to have good facts behind him, and I know he's a reputable writer because of his affiliation with the *New Yorker* as a staff writer. And I'm sure the *NYTimes* wouldn't publish something so accusatory out of the blue without some fact-checking.

What he's saying fits with what I've heard about friends' parents and grandparents getting hospital-borne infections—people say that a hospital is one of the most unhealthy places to be! So a procedure that reduces infections to the extent that Gawande says the checklist does, or did, has to be a good thing.

His argument that the checklist study should not have been stopped because it wasn't an experimental procedure makes a lot of sense to me.

Doubt Can this really be right? Here are my questions and doubts:

- Can government bureaucrats really be this unreasonable?
- Even more important, can it be true that so many doctors don't wash their hands and put on sterile gowns and gloves before inserting IVs? Enough to reduce infections from IV lines by 2/3 when they do?

Other issues:

- His attitude bothers me a little—he's so *sure*! Is his language covering something up? He's a little too blustery for my taste when he calls the gov't reasoning "blinkered" and "bizarre." I'm more inclined to believe arguments from people who are calm and methodical.
- I also wonder if an act of Congress is needed to let the research about the checklist resume. It IS research, I notice—he says so. So maybe it does need to have special oversight. I know that when we volunteered to participate in "experiments" in psych class we had to sign consent forms, even though all we were doing was answering questions. So maybe it does need to have special oversight?

Also, is the situation really as dire as he says? Can't doctors and hospitals use checklists to ensure good procedures anyway, without the research studies? Are lives really at risk?

Interviewing the Author

Another strategy for exploring your reactions to a text is to imagine interviewing the author and brainstorm the questions you might ask. This strategy enables you to identify the text's hot spots for you. These might be places where you want the author to clarify something, expand on something, or respond to your own objections or counterviews. Here are some questions Abby listed for Gawande.

Abby's Interview Questions

1. I am interested to know what has happened with the checklist studies since your op-ed was published. Has there been progress since the presidential administration changed? Or are you still trying to get Congress to take action?

2. You mentioned that you are working with the World Health Organization on the checklist. They can move forward with it despite the U.S. order to stop the research, can't they?

3. Can't individual doctors and hospitals develop their own checklists and procedures to safeguard patients from these infections?

4. You said that infections from IV lines were reduced by two-thirds when the checklist was in use. What proportion of hospital-borne infections overall does that represent? What are some other causes of people getting sicker while they are in the hospital than they were when they went in? What else can we do, as patients or as citizens asking Congress to act, to make hospitals safer?

Writing a Rhetorical Analysis Paper: Guidelines and an Example

A rhetorical analysis paper is the written counterpart of rhetorical reading. Writing this kind of paper gives you the opportunity to draw together and apply all the listening and questioning strategies discussed in this and the previous chapter for a twofold purpose: (1) articulating your own insights about how a text seeks to influence its readers, and (2) communicating those critical insights to other readers. Here, we offer general guidelines for writing a rhetorical analysis paper, followed by a student example. Abby's assignment is in the box on page 93.

Guidelines for Writing a Rhetorical Analysis

Getting Started

We suggest you prepare for your rhetorical analysis by undertaking at least two of the following preliminary activities:

1. Write a summary of the text you are going to analyze to make sure that you understand it well enough to represent its meaning accurately and fairly.

2. Make a descriptive outline as a way of scrutinizing distinctions between what the text says and what it does to develop those ideas.

3. Write a rhetorical précis of the text. (See pp. 62–63 for instructions.)

4. To identify a strong response or significant effect the text had on you as a reader, try one of the three activities on pages 89–91 for exploring your responses.

ABBY'S ASSIGNMENT

Write an essay of approximately 750 words (3 pages) in which you examine the key rhetorical strategies used by Atul Gawande in "A Lifesaving Checklist" to engage readers and convince them to adopt his perspective. Assume that members of your own **audience** are familiar with the rhetorical concepts discussed in this and earlier chapters, and that they have read the text you are analyzing, but have not thought carefully about it. Your **purpose** is to offer these readers insights about how the text works rhetorically. Present a perspective that might not be obvious upon someone's first reading of the piece but that you have gleaned from your analysis of the text.

Selecting a Focus for Your Analysis

To write an effective rhetorical analysis, you will need to focus on some aspect of the text's rhetorical methods, an aspect that merits close examination or critique. We suggest one of two approaches. You can start deductively with the effect the text had on you as a reader—a strong positive or negative response, a tension or contradiction you found in the text, or some aspect of the text that confused or surprised you. If you begin with your response, you will need to analyze the text to discover the rhetorical features that account for this response. How do they work? Why are these features effective or ineffective? Alternatively, you can start inductively by identifying and then analyzing particularly striking rhetorical features. If you begin inductively, you will need to consider how these features work and to what effect. What new understanding of the text does your analysis reveal?

Whether you begin deductively or inductively, you will need to select specific rhetorical features to write about. Choose features that you consider particularly effective or ineffective, or in which you detect inconsistencies or tensions between two different appeals. To frame your analysis, choose among the questions about texts' rhetorical methods suggested throughout this chapter.

Drafting Your Paper

Once you have determined a focus, reread the text carefully to find specific examples of these features, taking notes on how they contribute to the effect you have identified. Use these notes to draft a working thesis that states the gist of the insights your rhetorical analysis will offer about the text's meaning and methods. You can revise and refine this working thesis after you draft the whole paper. In your final draft, the thesis should clearly introduce the new understanding that results from your analysis and indicate what that analysis says about the text's effectiveness or ineffectiveness.

The full draft of your paper should have the following elements:

1. An introduction that includes (a) a brief summary of the text, (b) contextual information about the text, and (c) your thesis about the text's rhetorical effect
2. A series of body paragraphs that develop the thesis by (a) discussing specific rhetorical features that produce the rhetorical effect and (b) providing specific textual evidence to back up your points
3. A conclusion that makes clear (a) why the new understanding that your paper presents is important, and (b) why the insights of your analysis are significant to other readers

An Annotated Rhetorical Analysis of "A Lifesaving Checklist"

Earlier in this chapter, we presented some of Abby's early writing as she explored how she would approach analysis of Atul Gawande's 2007 *New York Times* op-ed column calling for federal rule changes that would permit resumption of research on the effectiveness of medical checklists designed to regularize anti-infection procedures. We now present the paper in which she applies many of the questioning techniques presented in this chapter. In addition, we have annotated the paper to highlight her analytical and organizational strategies.

A Surprising Checklist

Abby begins with brief information about the article and asserts her response of "surprise." Abby has chosen a deductive focus (p. 93) for her analysis.

Details here support her point about surprise, and forecast the other two major points she will develop: clear reasoning and direct language. Asserts thesis about why the argument is effective.

1   For many *New York Times* readers, it must have been somewhat surprising to encounter Atul Gawande's December 30, 2007, op-ed article criticizing a little known U.S. government office for endangering lives when it ordered a halt to research on the effectiveness of a medical checklist. We expect *Times* op-eds to be about urgent aspects of politics and foreign policy, not checklists. But this article presents the surprising information that medical doctors need to be reminded to wash their hands before they put intravenous lines into patients, something that might be urgent after all. Gawande uses clear reasoning and direct language to convince readers that it is. The combination creates an effective argument that is full of energy and difficult to argue against.

The medical checklist, which has five steps, was designed by researchers who wanted to see if using it on a regular basis would reduce infection. Gawande's primary claim is that the federal Office for Human Research Protections (OHRP) made a bad decision when it ordered doctors in Michigan to stop researching the effectiveness of the checklist. He wants the research resumed, and ultimately suggests that Congress may need to step in.

2 First body paragraph provides foundation for her analysis, with a factual summary of the argument and background about the checklist.

Gawande comes across with a strong *ethos*, partly because of the biographical note indicating that he's a surgeon, a *New Yorker* staff writer, and a book author. Appearing on the *New York Times* op-ed page lends him plenty of credibility, too. This authority grows through the concise, down-to-earth way that he presents facts, including lots of statistics. He starts out almost casually, setting the scene as if to tell a story. He mentions an obscure building where OHRP does its assigned work to protect people. "But lately you have to wonder," the doctor calmly notes (par. 1).[4] It may not seem like a serious life-or-death matter is coming up, but it is.

3 Second body paragraph examines Gawande's credibility as author and his establishment of a "down-to-earth" *ethos*.

Gawande gains momentum when he reports the "stunning" (positive) results of using the checklist: a large decrease in infections and thus a big increase in saved lives and saved money (par. 3). Then, the beginning of the next paragraph is just as stunning. We learn that OHRP stopped the study. The problem, it said, was that any research project involving humans requires everyone involved (patients and health care providers alike) to sign a consent form. But not everyone had, or could.

4 Abby's organization follows the flow of the op-ed, pointing out the strength of the reasoning within Gawande's unfolding argument.

Here is the core of both the government's argument and Gawande's rebuttal. OHRP says that doing research without informed consent violates scientific ethics. Gawande suggests, but never quite says exactly, that stopping the research on the checklist's usefulness violates

5 Abby pinpoints Gawande's central claim as a rebuttal of the government claim.

---

[4]Instead of using page references in her parenthetical citations of quotations, Abby is following her teacher's request to use the paragraph numbers in the reprint at the end of this chapter.

scientific ethics. In his final paragraph, he almost says it when he asserts that the OHRP authorities are "in danger of putting ethics bureaucracy in the way of actual ethical medical care" (par. 11). His next assertions are even more direct. First, he calls for the research to continue "unencumbered." Then, in his final sentence, he says that if the agency won't allow this to happen, "Then Congress will have to" (par. 11). It almost sounds like a threat of punishment.

Having worked through the article, Abby briefly states her understanding of Gawande's purpose and audience, points 3 and 4 in the rhetorical précis structure (p. 63).

6 Gawande's rhetorical purpose is to inform the general public and draw it to his cause. His target audience seems to be a combination of experts (and policymakers) with different levels of awareness and concern about the stopped research, and ordinary readers who want hospitals to be safer places.

Abby now steps back to analyze the way Gawande uses pathos to draw in the audience. Here, she analyzes the impact of Gawande's language on readers, especially nonexperts.

7 Gawande reaches out to the interests and values of both groups in this audience not only through reasoning, or *logos*, but by grabbing our attention through casual, conversational language. He got my nonexpert attention in the second paragraph with the surprising information that the checklist leads doctors to "actually wash their hands." It's shocking, yet it clicks with common knowledge that hospitals can make you sicker because they are home to so many dangerous germs. Soon the reader comes upon colloquial zingers such as "the results were stunning" (par. 3) and Gawande calling OHRP's decision "bizarre and dangerous" (par. 5). At first, this strong language may seem easy for a reader to resist. After all, we are taught in school to be suspicious of arguments that come on too strong. But the clarity of Gawande's reasoning is convincing.

Based on her analysis of ethos, pathos, and language, Abby unpacks Gawande's key moves in countering the OHRP position.

8 Labeling as "blinkered logic" the government's claim that informed consent was needed for research about the checklist (par. 5), Gawande proceeds to take apart the OHRP reasoning. (The phrase "blinkered logic" brought to my mind the image of big draft horses wearing those

big leather contraptions that keep them from seeing sideways. They can only see in one direction.) Gawande shows that the reasoning by analogy that considers testing a checklist to be ethically the same as testing a drug is just wrong. According to him, testing a checklist falls into the category of establishing minimum standards for the sake of safety, not the risky category of developing something new. The research on checklists is important, he continues, "not merely because it poses lower risks [than experimental drugs], but because a failure to carry it out poses a vastly greater risk to people's lives" (par. 6).

Abby points to "reasoning by analogy" as the core of Gawande's argument.

Gawande's careful rebuttal is all the more effective because he places it between strong assertions about the improvements that occurred when checklist standards were followed (par. 2–3) and the dire consequences of doctors not following minimum standards (par. 7–9). Early in the article, he uses everyday language to describe results: "they actually wash their hands and don a sterile gown and gloves" (par. 2). After he presents his argument that the government's reasoning is wrong, the language is much stronger: "a large body of evidence … has revealed a profound failure by health care professionals to follow basic steps proven to stop infection" (par. 7). Paragraph 2 takes readers into the reality of a hospital room; paragraph 7 passes judgment on what goes wrong.

9 Much of Abby's analysis has been based on the flow of reading the essay, preparing her own readers to see the strategic importance of organization in Gawande's argument, which she brings up explicitly in this paragraph.

10. By the end of this short article, a matter that seemed unlikely to concern an ordinary college student like me became surprisingly urgent, something that perhaps I should email Congress about. Gawande's success in the piece illustrates how effective an argument can be when it speaks in plain language directly to the interests of an audience, even an initially unconcerned audience. After all, evidence of "profound failure" in the health care system is difficult for anyone to brush away as insignificant.

10 Concluding paragraph ties the analytic threads together by commenting on how Gawande convinced this writer of his argument's importance.

Chapter Summary

This chapter has laid out for you a variety of strategies for questioning texts and composing your response to them, processes that involve carefully interrogating a text's argument and methods in order to critique it and join its conversation. We explained questioning strategies for examining

- A writer's credibility
- An argument's reasoning and logic
- A writer's strategies for engaging an audience and appealing to its interests and emotions
- A writer's language
- A text's ideology
- A text's use of visual elements

The discussion of visual images as elements of argument described how visuals could enhance a verbal text's appeal to *ethos, logos,* and *pathos,* as well as stand alone as visual arguments.

We then explained three easy-to-use methods for exploring your own reactions to a text: (1) writing out before/after responses, (2) playing the believing and doubting game, and (3) imagining an interview with the author.

Finally, along with a sample rhetorical analysis paper, we offered guidelines for writing such papers, including stipulations about audience and purpose in an analysis assignment, along with tips for getting started, selecting a focus, and drafting. Abby's rhetorical analysis of Gawande's op-ed argument then illustrates how the questioning strategies described in this chapter can help you write a college-level rhetorical analysis.

ATUL GAWANDE

A Lifesaving Checklist

Surgeon and writer Atul Gawande is a widely known advocate of using checklists for complex projects in a wide variety of fields. He is Professor of Surgery at Harvard Medical School and Professor in the Department of Health Policy and Management at the Harvard School of Public Health. He serves as director of the World Health Organization's (WHO) Global Challenge for Safer Surgical Care, and in that capacity guided development of a safe surgery checklist that was published by WHO in June 2008. It was modeled on the checklist designed to reduce hospital infections that he discusses in the article below that was modeled after aviation procedures. The surgical protocol, distributed as a laminated card, was featured in a celebrated reunion episode of the television show *ER* in March 2009. Dr. Gawande served as a consultant to the script writers.

Dr. Gawande is also a staff writer for the *New Yorker* and the author of three acclaimed books: *Complications: A Surgeon's Notes on an Imperfect Science* (2002); *Better: A Surgeon's Notes on Performance* (2007), a *New York Times* bestseller; and *The Checklist Manifesto: How to Get Things Right* (2010), also a major bestseller. The son of two medical doctors, Dr. Gawande was born in 1965 in Brooklyn, New York. This op-ed piece was published in the *New York Times* on Sunday, December 30, 2007.

━━━━━ ● ━━━━━

1   In Bethesda, Md., in a squat building off a suburban parkway, sits a small federal agency called the Office for Human Research Protections. Its aim is to protect people. But lately you have to wonder. Consider this recent case.

2   A year ago, researchers at Johns Hopkins University published the results of a program that instituted in nearly every intensive care unit in Michigan a simple five-step checklist designed to prevent certain hospital infections. It reminds doctors to make sure, for example, that before putting large intravenous lines into patients, they actually wash their hands and don a sterile gown and gloves.

3   The results were stunning. Within three months, the rate of bloodstream infections from these I.V. lines fell by two-thirds. The average I.C.U. cut its infection rate from 4 percent to zero. Over 18 months, the program saved more than 1,500 lives and nearly $200 million.

4   Yet this past month, the Office for Human Research Protections shut the program down. The agency issued notice to the researchers and the Michigan Health and Hospital Association that, by introducing a checklist and tracking the results without written, informed consent from each patient and health-care provider, they had violated scientific ethics regulations. Johns Hopkins had to halt not only the program in Michigan but also its plans to extend it to hospitals in New Jersey and Rhode Island.

5   The government's decision was bizarre and dangerous. But there was a certain blinkered logic to it, which went like this: A checklist is an alteration in medical care no less than an experimental drug is. Studying an experimental

drug in people without federal monitoring and explicit written permission from each patient is unethical and illegal. Therefore it is no less unethical and illegal to do the same with a checklist. Indeed, a checklist may require even more stringent oversight, the administration ruled, because the data gathered in testing it could put not only the patients but also the doctors at risk—by exposing how poorly some of them follow basic infection-prevention procedures.

6   The need for safeguards in medical experimentation has been evident since before the Nazi physician trials at Nuremberg. Testing a checklist for infection prevention, however, is not the same as testing an experimental drug—and neither are like-minded efforts now under way to reduce pneumonia in hospitals, improve the consistency of stroke and heart attack treatment and increase flu vaccination rates. Such organizational research work, new to medicine, aims to cement minimum standards and ensure they are followed, not to discover new therapies. This work is different from drug testing not merely because it poses lower risks, but because a failure to carry it out poses a vastly greater risk to people's lives.

7   A large body of evidence gathered in recent years has revealed a profound failure by health-care professionals to follow basic steps proven to stop infection and other major complications. We now know that hundreds of thousands of Americans suffer serious complications or die as a result. It's not for lack of effort. People in health care work long, hard hours. They are struggling, however, to provide increasingly complex care in the absence of effective systematization.

8   Excellent clinical care is no longer possible without doctors and nurses routinely using checklists and other organizational strategies and studying their results. There need to be as few barriers to such efforts as possible. Instead, the endeavor itself is treated as the danger.

9   If the government's ruling were applied more widely, whole swaths of critical work to ensure safe and effective care would either halt or shrink: efforts by the Centers for Disease Control and Prevention to examine responses to outbreaks of infectious disease; the military's program to track the care of wounded soldiers; the Five Million Lives campaign, by the nonprofit Institute for Healthcare Improvement, to reduce avoidable complications in 3,700 hospitals nationwide.

10   I work with the World Health Organization on a new effort to introduce surgical safety checklists worldwide. It aims to ensure that a dozen basic safety steps are actually followed in operating rooms here and abroad—that the operating team gives an antibiotic before making an incision, for example, and reviews how much blood loss to prepare for. A critical component of the program involves tracking successes and failures and learning from them. If each of the hundreds of hospitals we're trying to draw into the program were required to obtain permissions for this, even just from research regulators, few could join.

11   Scientific research regulations had previously exempted efforts to improve medical quality and public health—because they hadn't been scientific. Now that the work is becoming more systematic (and effective), the authorities have stepped in. And they're in danger of putting ethics bureaucracy in the way of actual ethical medical care. The agency should allow this research to continue unencumbered. If it won't, then Congress will have to.

Using Rhetorical Reading for Researched Writing Projects

*The only way in which a human being can make some approach
to knowing the whole of a subject is by hearing what can be said
about it by persons of every variety of opinion and studying all
modes in which it can be looked at by every character of mind.*

—John Stuart Mill

As the opening epigraph suggests, wisdom emerges only through careful examination of many differing perspectives. Given the wonders of twenty-first-century digital technology, it is probably not literally possible to consider "every variety of opinion," but this same technology

---

This chapter will show you systematic and efficient techniques for using
rhetorical reading strategies to find reliable sources within the twenty-first
century's deluge of information. Specifically, you will learn:

- The definition of **information literacy** and skills for developing it
- A process called Question Analysis that will make your research more
  productive
- Important differences in publication and editing processes for different
  kinds of sources
- Distinctions between library databases and Web search engines
- Tips for finding and evaluating reliable sources by examining
  - Publication type
  - Relevance
  - Currency and scope
  - Credentials of authors, experts, publishers, and sponsors

To illustrate these processes, we include excerpts from the research log that the
student Jack prepared while working on the paper about ethanol in Chapter 6.

---

does make it easier to examine a wide range of perspectives and "characters of mind" than was possible even a decade ago. What remains applicable in Mill's admonition is the goal of forging new understandings and new knowledge through thoughtful interactions with the thinking and writing of others, including—perhaps, especially—those with whom we do not expect to agree. With that goal in mind, this chapter will show you how to apply the techniques of reading rhetorically to find and select materials for rhetorically effective academic papers in which you can extend the conversation about topics that are important to you.

Rhetorical Reading and Information Literacy

To meet the challenge of finding relevant, reliable sources for research projects, you can incorporate techniques for rhetorical reading into the productive techniques that fall under the conceptual umbrella of **information literacy**. Doing so will equip you well for making sense out of the glut of information available to us all in the twenty-first century.

Librarians define *information literacy* in terms of the following five skills, which provide a map of research activities that will lead to successful college papers:

1. Determine what kind of information is needed and how much
2. Access the information efficiently
3. Evaluate critically the information and its sources
4. Use the information effectively for a specific purpose
5. Access and use the information ethically and legally in light of economic, social, and legal issues about information use and sources

These techniques will help you work efficiently and leave you plenty of time for thoughtful writing about the information and ideas that you uncover. We cover the first three in this chapter, and the remaining two in Chapter 6. That chapter demonstrates practical techniques for incorporating source materials into your own writing so that your papers synthesize new meaning from your diverse sources, as well as credit those sources in accordance with academic conventions. We illustrate both discussions by following the work of Jack, the Midwesterner we first met in Chapter 1, who is interested in corn ethanol. His final paper, "Arguing on the Basis of Wishful Thinking: An Analysis of Multiple Perspectives on Corn-Based Ethanol," which appears at the end of Chapter 6, was written in response to the assignment in the following box.

Notice that the definition of *information literacy* begins not with retrieving information, or even searching for it, but with careful consideration of what information is needed to accomplish a writer's purposes. In other words, writers who are information literate are writers who undertake their actual research with more in mind than a generalized "topic." They begin by carefully working out a research question and a set of expectations about how they will recognize relevant, valuable answers. You need to do the same.

JACK'S ASSIGNMENT TO ANALYZE MULTIPLE PERSPECTIVES

For this paper, you are to extend the conversation about environmental problems and solutions by (1) **analyzing** (taking apart and examining) several different perspectives on some aspect of the public discussion, then (2) **using synthesis** (putting together) to assert **your** understanding of the connections and differences among these perspectives. Choose a topic that particularly interests you and that is complex enough to include more than two "pro-con" perspectives.

Your audience: People like your classmates and instructor, who have heard of the issue but haven't looked into it enough to understand its dynamics.

Your purpose: Fill in our lack of understanding so that we can see what makes this issue so difficult to resolve. Instead of trying to convince us who is right, provide us with insights and information that will allow us to follow the unfolding conversation.

Length: 4–6 pages. Use MLA in-text citations and a works cited list.

Of course, it is likely that as your research progresses you will need to revise your original question, narrowing or broadening it as you catch the drift of the ongoing conversation about it. (Many researchers—not only students!—find that they must narrow their initial questions significantly just to make their project feasible for the amount of time available and the number of pages allotted for an assignment.) Eventually, your modified question will become part of your paper's introduction. Combined with the answers you find, it will be the basis of your thesis statement that announces your paper's purpose.

But first you need the question. How else will you recognize good answers?

Formulating and Analyzing Questions

Knowing what you are looking for is an essential first step to successful research-based writing. Whether you are fulfilling an assignment for a first-year writing class or for a capstone seminar in your major, the initial step in your research process—the step before you begin searching for sources—must be articulating your purpose. What question do you want to find answers to and write about?

Think of research-based writing assignments this way: Your job is to conduct an inquiry, not to shop around for sources. We offer a cautionary tale. Consider what went wrong when a student we'll call Phoebe treated a research assignment as a hunt for bargains instead of an inquiry. She was assigned to examine the potentially negative consequences of something that interested her. She had heard that Barbie dolls were being redesigned to have more natural proportions, so she thought Barbies would be an interesting "topic." She skipped the assigned step of writing out an initial question because, as she wrote in a later reflection, she thought that because Barbie was in the news, it would be faster just to search a periodicals database and see "what there was to say." She found so many articles that she felt overwhelmed, so she just chose the first three for which full text was available. This was not a good idea.

The resulting paper amounted to a patchwork of quotes and paraphrases from source materials stitched together by Phoebe's engaging descriptions of her own dolls. But it didn't synthesize her research sources, make a point, or reveal any conclusions that Phoebe had reached through research. To meet a page limit, Phoebe had merely interspersed stories about her own Barbies among three long summaries, first of a feminist's reflections about her childhood dolls, then of a psychological report about connections between gender stereotypes and eating disorders, and finally a commentary about the negative impact of Teen Talk Barbie's dislike for math class. She provided no analysis of Barbie's proposed new figure, the original topic, nor did she synthesize perspectives from her sources. Phoebe had been working without a sense of purpose during her research reading, with the result that her paper provided no new insights for readers.

Establishing Your Purpose

In our discussion of authors' purposes in Chapter 2, we stressed the importance of reading in a way that weighs your purpose as a reader against a given author's purpose for writing. Authors seek to change their readers' thinking in some way, we said, and we stressed that you, the reader, are the one who decides how much your thinking will change (p. 10).

The same dynamic applies when you undertake a research-based writing project. In an academic setting, the audience and genre are given: you are to write for an instructor according to the conventions of that discipline, very likely in response to an assignment prompt that narrows your range of subject matter. But beyond the need to satisfy a certain assignment, your real purpose, the question you seek to answer in your paper, is yours to determine. Your need for an answer is where the work on your paper begins. That need for an answer is what we called an "exigence" back in Chapter 2, the rhetorical term for a flaw or gap in knowledge that your efforts at research and writing will seek to remedy.

In the past, you may have encountered research assignments that expected you to 'do little more than report on a topic by gathering information and funneling it into paragraphs (like Phoebe did for the Barbie paper). However, the expectations and standards of your college teachers who assign papers with research components will be quite different—even in first-year writing courses. Your instructors will expect you to pose questions and provide not only answers but, in the language of our service economy, "value-added" content that demonstrates your own thinking. The value that you add will result from your work analyzing, organizing, and generally making sense out of the disconnected array of available information that you initially encounter.

Using Question Analysis to Plan a Research Strategy

A helpful strategy for conducting the multilayered process of researching, reading, and writing is a technique called **Question Analysis (QA)**, which offers a series of analytical prompts as a start-up routine for a research project.[1] These prompts, presented in Table 5.1, will not only help you recognize what you

TABLE 5.1 ● PROMPTS FOR QUESTION ANALYSIS	
Freewrite responses to these questions *before* you begin searching for sources.	
Questions to Ask	**Details for Follow-Up**
1. What question do you plan to investigate—and hope to answer—in this paper?	Avoid questions with obvious or simple answers.
2. What makes this question worth pursuing—to you and to others?	What benefits will come from answering the question, or from discovering why it is so difficult to answer?
3. What kind of expert would be able to provide good answers or the current best thinking about possible answers?	Perhaps a physician? Wildlife biologist? Water resource engineer? Journalist who has reported extensively on the subject?
4. Where do you expect to find particularly good information about this matter?	General interest publications? Specialized publications? Are you aware of a specific source with relevant material?
5. How recent must materials be to be relevant? What factors might make information outdated?	Defining a particular timeframe will help you search more efficiently. You may need information recorded before or after a particular event, such as an election or announcement of important medical findings. For situations that change rapidly, even a few months could make a difference.
6. What individuals or interest groups have a major stake in answering your question in a particular way?	For example, players' unions and sports team owners look at salary caps from different perspectives; lumber companies and environmental activists evaluate the effectiveness of the Endangered Species Act differently.
7. What kinds of bias do you need to be especially alert for on this particular question?	Bias of some kind is unavoidable, so it's important to recognize how it is operating in your sources so that you can compensate by consulting additional sources.
8. What words or phrases might be useful for some initial searching?	Different library databases often favor different search terms, so be prepared to consult with a librarian if you are not finding what you expect.

---

[1]The term *Question Analysis* comes from the work of academic librarian Cerise Oberman, who first broached it in "Question Analysis and the Learning Cycle," *Research Strategies* 1 (1983): 22–30. Print.

QUESTION ANALYSIS WORK EXCERPTED FROM JACK'S RESEARCH LOG

Question Analysis

1. My question: What are the advantages and disadvantages of developing corn-based ethanol? Will it become a clean substitute fuel for gasoline? (Uncle Johnny) Or is it too resource-intensive to produce to be profitable? (Uncle Clyde) I don't want to get into the "food v. fuel" debate—or energy independence. I just want to focus on what the current thinking is about corn and ethanol.

2. Why my question is worth pursuing: Because finding clean alternatives to gasoline is a high priority in the U.S. and around the world!

3. Experts I need: Scientists (chemists) in this field, journalists with a good overview, automakers, maybe economists.

4. Sources I think will have good info: Special issue of news magazine (?), Web sites for ethanol producers and environmentalists (Sierra Club, Concerned Scientists—get right name, automakers, *NY Times* or *Wall Street Journal*)

5. Time frame: Sources have to be pretty current for both political and scientific reasons, especially since January 2012, when the federal subsidies ended.

6. People with a stake in this: ethanol producers, environmentalists, automakers, farmers (pro and con), politicians (maybe not so much anymore—I have to see).

7. Bias to watch for: Some people are going to make money and some are going to lose. Probably every "expert" has a stake in it one way or the other.

8. Search terms: ethanol, biofuels (what are other types of biofuel?)

already know about possible answers to your research question, but will also suggest in advance what you need to "listen" for when you begin examining sources. The QA process of freewriting in response to these prompts will enable you (1) to make a preliminary map of the terrain you need to cover in your search for relevant source materials, and (2) to consider in advance what kinds of sources are going to be most useful for you to retrieve, read, and eventually integrate into your paper.

The QA process takes you out of a passive role (waiting to see what you can find) and puts you in charge of your research. Taking a small bit of time to prepare for research by using Question Analysis is similar to pausing to assess your background knowledge, an important part of preparing to read, as we described in Chapter 3 (pp. 41–42). The time spent planning and predicting will help you read more powerfully and thus choose potential sources more efficiently. Whatever your purpose for research, if you clarify your questions for yourself in advance, you will greatly reduce the risk of losing sight of your purpose once you dive into the search process. In fact, students who use QA for the first time are often surprised to discover how much they already know about where they are likely to find relevant sources and what issues those sources will raise. For additional insights into the QA process, we invite you to examine the excerpts from Jack's research log on the previous page.

Tips for Finding Reliable Sources

One of the great advantages of digital library resources is that they allow you to answer many questions about a source's reliability before you retrieve the actual source. That is, the same catalog and database screens that help you locate materials will likely also help you quickly evaluate the reliability and relevance of a potential source. That evaluation will in turn help you make good decisions about how far you want to pursue retrieval of that source. (Will you look at full text? Bookmark the source for later? Skim it online? Print it? Take notes? And so forth.)

The tips we provide in this section will help you use the QA questions efficiently to choose the sources you want to look at more closely. In the next section, we provide tips for evaluating the sources you choose to examine further. To illustrate how one student's research process unfolded, we include more excerpts from Jack's research log on pages 115 and 116.

Tip #1. Prefer Sources That Have Undergone Solid Editorial Review and Fact-Checking

Whether you access sources on paper in the library stacks or electronically through a library database or Web search engine, you must scrutinize their contexts and purposes for relevance and reliability. We recommend searching your library's online catalog and periodicals databases before jumping on the Web, which contains garbage as well as gold. The abundance and immediacy of information now available through the Internet make careful scrutiny crucial to your research work, especially during the early stages of your research, when your main goal is to catch the drift of the published conversation relevant to your research question. It can be difficult to assess the credibility of Web authors or the motives of a site sponsor, but here is a valuable rule of thumb: Whether you are reading in print or online, the more that you feel like someone is shouting and the more that ads interfere with your reading, the more cautious you need to be. For academic papers, you need sources with a calm, even-handed approach.

After filling out his Question Analysis log, Jack started his search the way librarians recommend, by looking for current magazine and journal articles in a periodicals database. The materials found through these databases are easy to access, efficient to use, and more current than books, which take a long time to write and manufacture. Furthermore, the editorial processes at the newspapers, magazines, and journals indexed in the databases are typically rigorous. Such editing represents major investments of time and money. It involves multiple readers, fact-checking, quote-checking, and even background-checking of quoted sources. With so many people not only checking content but staking their professional reputations on quality and credibility, such materials clearly deserve preference.

Jack knew that his research about ethanol would have to include advocacy sites on the Web, from both ethanol producers and ethanol skeptics. But he also knew that the diversity of opinion made it all the more important that he find reliable, edited sources that could provide recent discussions. He knew that although even reputable journalists might favor one perspective over another, if they want to get their stories in print and if they want to have continued access to their sources, they need to report all points of view fairly. In the end, he brought in pro-ethanol advocates primarily through news sources and used just one anti-ethanol source directly from the Web site of an organization referred to in a *New York Times* article. (See paragraph 6 of Jack's paper.)

Library Databases and Web Search Engines

Library databases (such as ProQuest or Lexis-Nexis) and Web search engines (such as Google, Yahoo!, and Bing) will lead you to significantly different types of material because they search different parts of the Internet.[2] Libraries pay substantial subscription fees for the password-protected database services that give you access to electronic archives of print periodicals—magazines, trade journals, scholarly journals, and major newspapers. "We pay for quality," librarians at public and university libraries commonly stress. In contrast, Web search engines access the free-access part of the Internet. You can use these search engines without charge because their revenue comes from advertisers. Within seconds they will accumulate for you an overwhelming number of potential sources, many of them unreliable, unrelated to your purposes, and probably redundant. Indeed, even those links that do appear helpful might no longer be working, or might take you to a Web site where that promising article or report is no longer available. Remember this: the search engine algorithms that measure popularity are not good measures of reliability.

In contrast, initiating a search in a library subscription database sets off a search of the indexes and archives of sources recommended by experienced researchers and experts in a wide variety of fields. The focus is primarily on print sources, but some databases now index materials from radio and TV broadcasts and reputable blogs. See, for example, the "source types" in Figure 5.1, the "Easy Search" screen of the LexisNexis database. In addition, audio and video materials are frequently archived and indexed through the Web sites of television and radio networks, most notably National Public Radio and the *PBS NewsHour* (sources that Jack found helpful).

As our last point about TV and radio resources should confirm, we are not recommending that you shun material published on the Web. Doing so would

---

[2]We follow the practice of using "Internet" to refer to the entire network of linked computers around the world and "Web" to refer to material available through the graphical interface used by browsers such as Firefox, Internet Explorer, Safari, Chrome, and so forth.

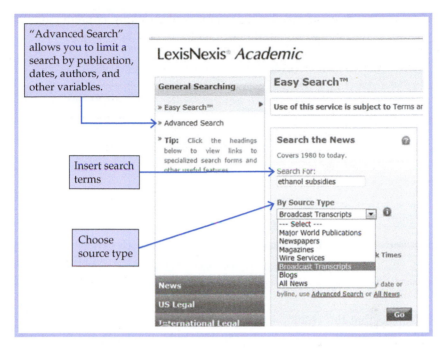

FIGURE 5.1 Close-up view of a LexisNexis "Easy Search" screen showing types of sources available

be a big mistake. Jack needed to know what was being said on the Web sites of ethanol advocates as well as environmental activists. Many Web materials have undergone rigorous editorial processes; furthermore, highly reputable print periodicals often publish major articles on the Web. Some sites, such as *nytimes. com*, have far more resources available on the Web than in print editions. Nonetheless, for consistent reliability as well as for the sake of efficiency in searching and evaluating, we recommend starting with periodicals to which your library subscribes through a database.

Some specialized databases are available only on CD-ROM in the library itself, but the extensive databases of general interest materials are stored on computers that may be miles away from the library. While these computers are conducting your search, they might also be conducting a search on behalf of your best friend from home, who is attending school in another state. When you use these databases from campus, they may seem to be as free of cost as a Web search engine; however, be assured that libraries do pay substantial subscription fees to the database companies. That is why access to them is password-protected and why access is typically restricted from off campus.

Periodicals databases are indexed according to traditional bibliographic categories (author, article title, publication title, etc.) as well as by specialized key words connected to subject matter. When you enter your search terms, the database checks these indexed categories along with article abstracts and key

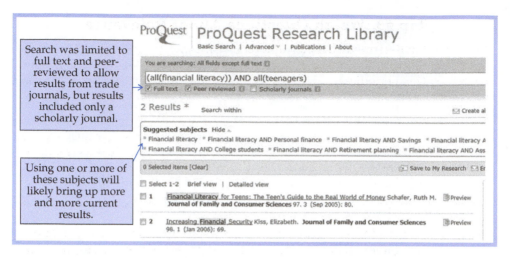

FIGURE 5.2 Close-up view of a screen showing results from a ProQuest Research Library search for "financial literacy AND teenagers" and providing alternate subject terms

word lists so that the results screen can suggest additional search terms and combinations, as Figure 5.2 illustrates. Both sets of results are usually much smaller and more manageable than those produced by Web searches. Furthermore, as you will see in the section on evaluating sources beginning on page 112, rhetorical readers can pick up important evaluative cues from search results. One note of caution: manipulating subject terms and doing advanced searches can become complex and frustrating. If you are not getting the results you expect, ask a librarian for help.

Tip #2. Appreciate the Value of Specialized Periodicals for General Audiences

Your ability to understand your sources will be important to the success of your project, so finding material written at a suitable level of expertise must be a priority. You can count on being able to read general interest publications comfortably, but if they seem oversimplified (perhaps even sensationalized), or if they don't provide the depth of information you are looking for, consider searching within a newsstand periodical that provides in-depth discussion for the general public on more specialized topics, for example, *American Health*, *Money*, *Psychology Today*, *Consumer Reports* (very useful to Jack), or one of our favorites, the *Chronicle of Higher Education*. These can be good places for a student researcher to find extended but readily understood material. Be forewarned, however: The more specialized the publication, the greater the likelihood that you will find it difficult to understand, either because the material is too technical or because the author assumes readers are more familiar with the subject than you happen to be. If you find that your question has been addressed only at high levels of scholarship, you will probably need to revise it.

Tip #3. Weigh Questions About Relevance

You can often determine the relevance of a source to your project just by examining the bibliographic information provided in library catalogs (for books) and databases (for periodicals).[3] Use the bibliographic information to answer the following three basic questions about a source's purpose and method:

1. **What ideas and information does this text offer?** Examine the title, subtitle, and abstract. Does the information indicate what kind of source it is (scholarly, trade, etc.)? You can make good guesses about an article's approach and intended audience on the basis of what you already know or can discern from the periodical and article titles. For books, a table of contents may be available in the online catalog along with the name of the publisher.

2. **Can I trust the source of information?** Again consider what you know or can gather about the credentials and reputation of the author, publisher, or Web sponsor. Remember that university presses are particularly reliable. On the Web, click the Home and About Us tabs for information about the site sponsor (now required information for Modern Language Association [MLA] citations). If there is no evidence of a reputable site sponsor, do not use the source.[4] (Note: Material from an individual's home page is not usually acceptable for academic papers, no matter how impressive it may appear. Links from such pages may uncover useful and reliable sources, however).

3. **Will I be able to understand what the source says—was it written for someone at my level of expertise?** Draw inferences about the intended readers from the title, publisher's reputation, and an abstract or table of contents, then spot read as needed. If the article is full of technical material, concentrate on making sense of the abstract and conclusions sections.

Tip #4. Ask a Librarian

Librarians know where to find things and how to narrow searches. They can tell you which database to look in to find local news coverage of the effects of the emerald ash borer beetle, for example, and they usually know which database offers full-text articles from a certain journal and which offers only abstracts. Some journals and magazines are selective about the databases to which they provide access, or full-text access, and librarians will know which database is the best to consult for different types of subject matter. They also can offer good suggestions for trade publications related to something that interests you, or for alternate subject/search terms, such as "capital punishment" versus "death penalty," including which database uses which term.

---

[3] For Web sources, it is important that you examine the actual source, not just the link supplied by the search engine.

[4] By "site sponsor" we mean the organization behind the Web page, not advertisers on it.

Tips for Evaluating Sources

Once you have narrowed down a list of potential sources, the tips and questions in this section will guide your evaluation of texts you are considering as possible sources and will help you use your rhetorical reading skills to infer the original context and purpose of potential sources. The two over-reaching issues are these:

- How will a given source help you answer your research question?
- How can you use the source in your own writing?

Tip #5. Read the Abstracts and Conclusions Sections of Scholarly Articles

In the academic world, the most highly regarded periodicals are **peer-reviewed journals**, also known as **refereed journals** and **scholarly journals**.[5] These journals only publish articles that have been approved by several experts as meeting high scholarly standards and contributing to new knowledge. They rarely publish advertisements. These high levels of credibility make such journals excellent sources for college papers. Their drawback is that material written for experts and scholars may be difficult for readers outside the field to understand. However, even if you cannot understand all the details in material from scientific journals such as the *New England Journal of Medicine* or *JAMA,* reading the abstract, background, and conclusions sections of a given study may provide you with better insights about the complexities of the findings than will a short news report.

Tip #6. Examine a Text's Currency and Scope

Take your initial evaluation further by using bibliographic information about date of publication and length to judge how usable the material may be for your purposes. Abstracts may help you catch a publication's tone and scope, but you can get better information by spot reading in the full text, which will help you judge the intended audience. In library databases, examining a PDF version of the article, if available, is ideal because the images of actual pages from the periodical will reveal layout, illustrations, and advertisements, all cues to the publication's genre and audience. If PDF is not available in the database you are using, try another of your library's periodicals databases. In some cases, you may have to go to the stacks to find paper copy to skim in order to determine

---

[5]The glossary for the library subscription database ProQuest distinguishes between "peer-reviewed" journals and "scholarly" journals, limiting *scholarly* to journals written by and for academics and published by professional associations or university presses. Most articles (but not all) in scholarly publications are peer-reviewed, as are articles in many trade publications.

whether a source that seems promising will actually be valuable for your purposes. (Note: We caution you not to rely solely on any database's abstract in place of the source itself. They are often written by nonexperts who may leave out important facts and context, or who may be sloppy about indicating when they are quoting or the extent to which they are paraphrasing. Any of these factors could lead to embarrassment for you, or worse.)

Use the following questions as a guide:

1. **How current is the source in relation to your research question?** You will usually want the most recent information available, but if you are researching a historical phenomenon, "current" must be balanced with "relevant," and thus does not necessarily mean "recent."

2. **How extensive is the source? How much detail is present? What kind of evidence is used?** A twenty-page article contrasting American and Japanese management styles might be just what you need, or it might be far too detailed for your purposes. A cheery three-paragraph piece in *Glamour* or *GQ* about the value of regular dental checkups might enable you to make a point about the treatment of dental hygiene in popular magazines, but it won't tell you much about the affordability of dental care.

Tip #7. Check Authors' and Experts' Basis of Authority

Your background knowledge about subject matter and sources will often help you answer questions about an author or expert's trustworthiness. When you need more information, skim the source for information, look for a biographical note about the author (possibly elsewhere in the publication or on the Web site), or try other available search tools. Once you have selected certain materials to read in depth for your project, use them to consider the following questions about credibility:

1. **What are the author's credentials and qualifications regarding the subject?** See what you can learn about this person's professional expertise. (You may start recognizing names that come up regularly.) Is the writer an expert in the field? A journalist who writes about the subject frequently? An abstract or a note at the end of a full-text article may supply biographical information. A quick search by author (perhaps via a click on the name) will show you what this person has written recently for the same periodical. You might discover, for example, that the author of a piece on rap music is not an expert on rap or hip-hop but does regularly write about the business side of the entertainment industry. This discovery may signal that the article is not likely to help you if you want to write about rap music's roots in the African-American folk tradition, but if you are interested in how rap has been marketed over the years or how it fits into the larger entertainment market, additional articles by this author may lead to just what you need.

2. **What are the credentials and qualifications of experts who are cited?** In general-circulation periodicals (newspapers and newsmagazines), the writer's expertise is probably less important than is the expertise of the sources interviewed. Gathering information about the people quoted in an article usually requires skimming to see what background information is supplied. Using a database to look for material written by those experts can lead to more in-depth sources and confirm their reputations.

3. **What can you tell about the writer's or expert's political views or affiliations that might affect his or her credibility?** You are more likely to uncover this information in the text than in the citation. (Much of the time you will have to use your rhetorical reading skills to infer the writer's ideology—see Chapter 4.) If the purpose of your paper dictates that you need to find out more about a writer's ideological biases, a quick search in *Books in Print*, in a biography database, or on the Web will probably tell you what you need to know. You might learn, for example, that a particular writer recently received an award from the American Civil Liberties Union (on the left) or the Heritage Foundation (on the right), or you might discover that a medical expert interviewed about the dangers of plastic surgery is a well-known celebrity doctor. It will be up to you to determine the extent to which this information adds or detracts from the person's credibility in relation to your research questions and purposes.

Tip #8. Consider the Reputation of Publishers and Sponsors

Crucial information for evaluating a source can become apparent when you examine the purposes and motives of its publisher. Regardless of whether you access the source on paper or on the Web, it is important to consider how and why the material has become available in the first place. The following questions about audience, review process, and reputation will help round out your process of evaluating potential sources.

1. **What is the periodical's target audience—the general public or a specialized audience? Is it known for providing good information about the subject that interests you?** If you are researching antidepressants, for example, you will find that articles in popular magazines are often upbeat about their value. You'll probably find more reliable information about the side effects of drugs in specialized magazines or medically oriented journals.

2. **How extensive a review process did the article have to undergo before the text was published? Is it from a scholarly journal?** Increasing numbers of print periodicals, particularly newspapers, post material on the Web, and you can rely on their editorial processes regarding material found on their sites. Nevertheless, it's also important to remember that general circulation publications and news sites are driven by

marketplace concerns. Editors choose articles that will help sell copies (or draw eyeballs) because increases in circulation and clicks will increase advertising revenue. Beware of overstatement.

3. **Is the publisher or site sponsor known to have a viewpoint that might influence its coverage of material that is relevant to your question?** We have previously noted that books published by university presses can be assumed to be reliable, for example. Nonetheless, do be alert for political biases, not because you can avoid bias but because you may want to be sure to consult sources with different leanings. A wide variety of nonprofit, public service, and governmental entities have extensive and useful Web sites. Consider how an organization's mission may influence its Web presentations. If you use material from an organization known for supporting certain causes or positions, scrutinize it carefully for the effects of bias. If you let your own readers know relevant information about a source's reputation (something that might not be obvious), you will be demonstrating that you are knowledgeable about that reputation.

MORE EXCERPTS FROM JACK'S RESEARCH LOG

To illustrate how a student might apply these evaluation strategies to a research project, we conclude this chapter with more items from Jack's research log.

Evaluating Sources

1. **Update on My Searches**
   Searched for "ethanol" in ProQuest, the Web, and in "Times Topics" at *nytimes.com*. I found 100's of articles, and by spot reading or skimming them, I have discovered that my question is too simple. Uncle Clyde and Uncle Johnny are both right, but by going all out with corn hybridized for ethanol, Johnny is taking the bigger risk if the bottom falls out of the ethanol market because of oil prices or a bad economy. I had no idea there were so many organizations (lobbies, I guess) with a stake in this.

2. **Best Sources So Far**
   **Archive of a *Chronicle of Higher Education* online discussion with an Iowa State engineering professor about biofuels—his answers to questions give good information, but it's the questions themselves that are helping me focus. (Bookmarked—may print it so I can see it better.)

   Relevance? Provides great overview—I'm learning a lot from it that fits into the more news-based articles. Trustworthy, yes.

   Currency and Scope? Covers many bases, which is why I like it. It's from 2007, but I haven't found anything since that is as clear from the scientific POV. (Did talk to a librarian.)

   Author and experts quoted? Good—it's all from one academic expert, not an advocate. He seems cautious. Important quote: "Ultimately, we cannot

<u>achieve our goals through corn grain ethanol alone</u>." (I am underlining quotes to keep track of them.)

Publishers and Sponsors? The CHE is one of the sources the librarian mentioned when I asked for help after realizing that what was coming up online was very "inside update" stuff about green business—I could understand the words, but not the context. (Too many details!) The CHE target audience is professors, but ones who are NOT experts in whatever topic. I can understand this guy, AND the people asking him questions.

**Consumer Reports, "The Ethanol Myth." Found in Ebscohost.

Relevance? Good perspective because it's written for consumers. The "myth" aspect is that ethanol will solve everything. It's not anti-ethanol, just cautious and a good explainer.

Currency and Scope? Good-ish. 2006. Focuses on flex fuel vehicles. (They use E85, 85% ethanol, 15% gasoline; ordinary gasoline these days is 10% ethanol.)

Author and experts quoted? Based on their testing and research, so absolutely reliable—everybody knows that CR is a reliable source!

Economist, "Plagued by Politics." Linked from PBS page.

More recent (2011) than the CR piece, and the subtitle tells the story: "Biofuels are an example of what not to do." I know they tend to be lefties, but this has an international perspective and some good data.

3. **Worst Source So Far**

   You asked for it! The headline on the home page for *www.ethanolfacts.com* says "Ethanol is the answer to many of America's challenges. This is the place for the answers about ethanol." Great reasoning, eh? Do you think there will be anything negative about ethanol on this site? On the other hand, I guess I can learn from it how they spin the bad news. It's sponsored by the National Corn Growers Association, so they must mean "corn ethanol is the answer to America's challenges."
   ***

Still to Do

- I need to watch a news video online about alternate sources of ethanol that my professor recommended from the PBS NewsHour.
- Search NPR. Mom said she heard something there not long ago that corn for ethanol for fuel has gone beyond corn for food.
- MUST find an update about the impact of the subsidy ending. I found a great op-ed and letters responding to it, but it turned out it was all from before Congress finally voted the subsidies out.
- Keep checking the *NY Times* Green, Inc., bloggers for updates, and go back to Times Topics for the "ethanol" entry to check my details.

Chapter Summary

This chapter has described how rhetorical reading skills will help you succeed in two of your key tasks as a researcher: formulating questions and evaluating resources. Because college teachers expect students to demonstrate their own thinking about a given research question, successful academic papers are those in which the student's claims and commentary are more prominent than material from research sources.

To assist your pre-research and research processes, we discussed the following:

- The importance of approaching a research project with a clear sense of purpose and careful planning
- The skills needed to develop information literacy
- Question analysis (QA) prompts to use before you begin an active search for sources
- The differences between searching for sources through library subscription databases and through Web search engines
- The differences in publication and editing processes for different kinds of both print and Web sources

We offered tips for finding and using reliable sources, including consulting with a librarian, and recommended that you evaluate potential sources by asking specific questions about a potential source concerning its relevance to your project, its currency and scope, the background and reputation of authors and experts, and the credibility and likely biases of publishers and Web page sponsors.

To illustrate these processes, we provided excerpts from Jack's research log.

Making Knowledge: Incorporating Reading into Writing

The mind in action selects and orders, matches and balances, sorting and generating as it shapes meanings and controls their interdependencies.

—Ann E. Berthoff

I n this chapter we address one of the biggest challenges in college writing: incorporating other writers' texts into your own without letting them take over. The techniques we present here will help you foreground your sense of purpose and thus help you author strong, rhetorically effective texts. As we

In this chapter you will learn:
- How to use material from your reading to extend and develop your own points
- How to make the distinction between your ideas (and words) and your sources' ideas (and words) absolutely clear to your readers
- How to manage your writing process
- How to avoid any hint of plagiarism by following guidelines for integrating summaries, paraphrases, and quotations into your work
- How to give credit where credit is due by using attributive tags and by following the Modern Language Association (MLA) guidelines for in-text citations. (The Appendix offers model citation formats.)

To illustrate many of these principles, we present at the end of the chapter Jack's MLA-formatted paper about corn-based ethanol.

have stressed in the preceding chapters, composing a text is an opportunity to add your voice to the ongoing conversation about a particular topic. Your readers, whether your peers or your professors, want to read what *you* have to say, not a rehash of what others have said.

Asserting Your Authority as a Reader and Writer

"I have nothing to say! It's all been said!" This lament is a familiar one. In the midst of a complicated reading and writing project, it is not unusual for any of us—students, teachers, or professional writers—to lose sight of our original goals and thus lose confidence that we have ideas worth writing about.

Throughout this book, we have argued that reading is an active, constructive process. We don't need to convince you that writing, too, is an active process; after all, to write, one must actually make words appear on a page or screen. Nevertheless, as we turn to the subject of connecting reading and writing, we need to warn you against **passive writing,** writing that just translates what is on someone else's page onto your page. Passive writing is packed full of summaries, paraphrases, and quotes (sometimes very lengthy quotes) but contains very little content from the writer. Writing that simply assembles other people's ideas but does not assert its author's reason for writing is not likely to give its audience a reason for reading.

Passive writing occurs when students get so immersed in reading published sources that they find it difficult to maintain their own sense of purpose as authors: they lose track of their **author-ity,** the state of being an **author.** Still worse, writers who are uncertain about a source text's content or purposes may begin to insert quotations or paraphrases into their own texts without clear purpose. Perhaps awed by the rush of facts and abstractions in materials they are reading, they yield their authority as both readers and writers to the previously published texts. They begin writing sentences that mouth the words of their sources, almost as a ventriloquist casts a voice into a dummy—but in this case, onto an inert page. In effect, these writers let themselves be silenced by the experts. Thus, they not only fail to gain their readers' confidence but they lose the opportunity to make their own contribution to the discussion.

As you work with the advice in this chapter, you will begin to discover a powerful truth: rhetorical reading leads to rhetorically powerful writing. Just as rhetorical reading involves analyzing and critiquing an author's method as well as content, rhetorically effective writing asserts its purpose and method along with its content. Strong writers use the knowledge and understanding gained from their reading to build their own authority so that they can, in turn, *author* their own texts. These strong texts will engage readers because they not only "say" clearly what they mean, but "do" what they intend: extend the conversation by providing information in a new way and asserting ideas that will alter their readers' view of the subject.

Managing Your Writing Process

To assert your authority as a writer, you need to think of writing as an active process of making new meaning, of adding your voice to an ongoing conversation about a subject. It is not just a matter of retrieving something that is fully formed in your own head or someone else's, nor is it a matter of finding other people's ideas to cobble together. Rather, it is a matter of finding a compelling reason to write—most often, a question worth exploring—then actively constructing a text that accomplishes that purpose.

Recognizing that the process of creating a text will vary from writer to writer and from situation to situation, we offer in this section a variety of strategies that will help you claim your own authority as a writer. Then, after we discuss different phases of developing a paper, we offer a number of highly practical tips in Table 6.1, "Strategies for Managing Your Writing Processes," on pages 124–127. The table follows the organization of our discussion in this section, from getting started and generating ideas to editing and polishing, including a section on "What to Do When You Get Stuck." We hope you will find the suggestions helpful. The table is designed so that you can refer to it whenever you want to nudge your writing or thinking processes forward as you are developing a paper.

Think of the strategies and processes we describe not as a series of steps to go through in a strictly linear fashion, but as a set of methods that is **recursive**— that is, these methods will enable you to curve back to revise and adjust earlier parts of a draft when you discover new angles or see a new way to refine how you stated important ideas.

Strategies for Getting Started

As a college writer, you are more likely to succeed when you can make an assignment your own. Instead of writing just to fulfill an assignment, you need to construct your own "take" on the subject. Imagine yourself writing to a real audience for a real purpose. To do this, create your own **exigence**—a term we first referred to back in Chapter 2 (p. 18) as part of explaining how important it is for rhetorical readers to analyze an author's purpose. When you take on the role of *writing* rhetorically, you must similarly focus on a purpose, this time your own intention to bring about some kind of change in your audience. Such changes can have a wide range—to correct a misunderstanding, to talk back to something someone else has said, to propose a solution to a problem, to explore and shed new light on an issue, to change your audience's thinking or attitudes, to make your audience appreciate something or value it differently, to call for action. Whether you are writing something long or short, thinking about how you want your readers to respond to your writing—your rhetorical aim—will help you come across more clearly.

Whatever kind of writing assignment you are given, the starting point of the writing process should be a problematic question or a risky claim. Although it might be tempting to start with ideas that are familiar or safe, that you are already firmly committed to or that are already settled in your mind, that approach usually leads to flat, perfunctory writing that fails to engage readers. The better approach is instead to start with a question that is genuinely puzzling to you, or with a tentative claim that provokes multiple perspectives and invites audience resistance or skepticism.

Strategies for Generating Ideas

Once you have identified a starting point, you will need to develop your ideas by analyzing more fully the single text you are writing about or by finding additional texts that can expand, deepen, and challenge your understanding of your research question. In either case, the rhetorical reading strategies in Chapters 3 and 4 should help you generate ideas. Remember that when you are writing to make a claim about a particular text (whether it is an assigned text or a research source you have found), it is important to re-read the text with your paper's starting point and purpose in mind. Be sure to note all the textual details you might use to support your own claim. Likewise, look for counterevidence that you may have missed on your first time through the text and that you will need to address in some way. Perhaps this counterevidence will cause you to qualify or soften your claim.

Conferencing with your teacher, peer group, or a writing center tutor is another good way to generate ideas for writing. When you try to explain your rough plans to someone else, it's likely you will discover new ideas along with connections that you didn't see before. Moreover, your conferencing partners will probably ask you questions that will trigger new lines of thinking or enable you to see gaps in your current thinking that may require further analysis or research. The questions listed in the first part of Table 6.1 (p. 124) are designed to help you discover such new approaches.

Strategies for Writing a First Draft

Good first drafts are usually messy, confusing, and imperfect. Fear of this messiness, or fear of the blank screen or page, often prevents writers from producing idea-generating early drafts and thus reduces the time available for multiple revisions. To get past such fears, think of your first draft as a **discovery draft.** Its purpose, in other words, is to extend the process of figuring out what you have to say and how to say it. You can work out some of the details later. A writer's most original ideas often appear in the final paragraph of these drafts, at the point where the writer finally recognized them. This is not a problem at the rough draft stage because your goal is simply to start working out ideas. On the next draft, you can move those ideas to a more prominent position in the paper as you reshape and refine your ideas.

STRUCTURE OF A CLASSICAL ARGUMENT

I. Introduction or *Exordium*
   Explains the significance of the issue
II. Narrative or *Narratio*
   Provides background information
   States the writer's thesis or claim
III. Partition or *Partitio*
   Maps the issues to be discussed
IV. Confirmation or *Confirmatio*
   Supports the claim through a sequence of reasons and evidence
V. Refutation or *Refutatio*
   Summarizes and responds to opposing views
VI. Conclusion or *Peroration*
   Calls for action and relates the argument to larger issues

If your paper assignment calls for a particular organizational format—such as a classical argument, a technical report, an evaluative review of literature—use that format as an idea-generating template for producing various parts of your text. The box above, for example, presents an outline for a classical argument. This kind of structure can help you build your first draft section by section. The specific requirements for each section will provide you with implicit questions to address in that section. When you write out the answers, you will have a discovery draft. You'll find good tips about drafting, including a helpful list of strategies for getting "unstuck," in Table 6.1 (p. 125).

Strategies for Evaluating Your Draft for Revision

Producing an initial draft is only the first step in producing a successful, polished paper. For most college assignments, success requires substantial revision through multiple drafts. Effective revision is not just minor repair or sentence correction but a matter of literally re-seeing a draft. This kind of re-seeing requires a critical distance that is not easy to achieve, so Table 6.1 offers specific techniques to help you see your text the way a reader might. As you gain experience as a writer, you will find that the urge to revise begins when you discover confusing passages, points that need more support or development, contradictions or flaws in thinking, gaps in your argument, places where the text fails to anticipate audience questions or objections, and so forth. Sometimes you will even decide to reword your thesis and reorganize.

TABLE 6.1 • STRATEGIES FOR MANAGING YOUR WRITING PROCESSES

Strategies for Getting Started

When responding to a text:

Establish your own response using key questions.

- Is the author credible? What proves her credibility?

- How is the author appealing to reason? What evidence does she provide?

- How is the author appealing to the reader's emotions, values, and interests? How can you tell?

- What language is the author using? What does that say about her intent?

- What visuals are included? How do they interact with the text?

- What does the text reveal about the author's ideology?

When exploring your own research question:

Brainstorm a list of questions or problems that intrigue you.

- Why does this question or problem matter? To whom?

- Do you expect to find agreement about answers? Uncertainty? Controversy?

- What do you expect to find as points of disagreement or uncertainty?

- What kinds of experts will have good answers?

- Where will you find good information?

- Who (individuals or interest groups) has a major stake in answering your question in certain ways?

What change do you want to bring about in *your* readers' thinking?

- What is your broad aim in this text you will write? Informing? Interpreting? Persuading? (See Table 2.1.)

- Why is this change in your audience's thinking important?

- Do you want readers to see an inconsistency or contradiction?

- Do you want to ensure readers aren't fooled by a ploy or faulty reasoning?

- Do you want to highlight the broad significance of a claim?

Strategies for Generating Ideas

When responding to a text:

Develop your ideas by analyzing the text you're writing about.

- Whose minds is the text trying to change, about what, and why?

- Whose minds are **you** trying to change, about what, and why?

- What information will help you establish your credibility?

- How can you make your readers concerned about your topic?

When exploring your own research question:

Develop your ideas by finding texts that will deepen and challenge your understanding of your question.

- How will a given source advance your purpose for writing?

- Does it provide background information?

- Does it provide a perspective on framing the discussion?

- Does it provide support for your claims?

- Does it provide a new perspective?

TABLE 6.1 ● STRATEGIES FOR MANAGING YOUR WRITING PROCESSES (CONTINUED)

Strategies for Generating Ideas (Continued)

- What kind of supporting evidence will be persuasive to your readers?
- What values or interests do you share with your readers?
- What differences in opinions or values might you need to try to overcome?

- Does the source provide a compelling example or illustration of a point?
- Does it provide solid evidence you can refer to?

Remember: Conferencing with your teacher, peer reviewers, or a writing center tutor can be a great way to generate ideas.

Strategies for Writing a First Draft

- Try to produce a complete first draft without worrying about perfection.
- Use formats for specific genres (e.g., a classical argument, lab report, literature review, etc.) to establish sections you can fill in.
- Create an outline with a bulleted list of important points you want to make.
- Use color, lines, and arrows to connect related ideas and source texts.
- If you have trouble with introductions, start somewhere else with a point you feel strongly about.
- Plan on rewriting your opening paragraph once you have a nearly complete draft.
- Turn off spelling and grammar checkers while you are drafting.

What to Do When You Get Stuck

- Make notes to yourself in caps about the problem ("NEED TRANSITION") and move on.
- If you have a vague idea but can't figure out how to say it, freewrite in caps or color, "WHAT I REALLY WANT TO SAY IS. . . ."
- Open a second file and complain there about why you are stuck. Moving away from your text is likely to help you figure out a solution.
- Silence your internal critic by turning off your computer monitor so you can't see what you're writing, then spill out your unpolished ideas. When you turn the screen back on, fill in gaps and straighten out the sentences.
- Try talking out your draft with someone who will take notes or record you. You can often discover what you have to say better by talking than by writing.

(continued)

TABLE 6.1 • STRATEGIES FOR MANAGING YOUR WRITING PROCESSES (CONTINUED)

Strategies for Evaluating Your Drafts for Revision

Techniques to Help You Adopt a Reader's Perspective

- Print your draft and read it from hard copy, annotating for problems and ideas for revision.

- Try to "listen" to your own text in some of the ways outlined in Chapter 3.
  - Make a descriptive outline of its major chunks.
  - Draw an idea map.
  - Write a rhetorical précis.

- For papers that call for a thesis-support structure, make sure your support paragraphs connect back to your thesis statement clearly and directly.

Strategies for Peer Response and Revision

Tips for Offering Feedback to Others

Respond honestly and productively.

- Address the writer's specific requests for feedback.
- Offer comments from a *reader's* perspective.
- Make sure that your comments are text-specific, not general.
- Identify specific points that were unclear and try to explain the questions they raised for you.
- Be selective. Choose only two or three major concerns to comment on in detail.
- Respond at the level of ideas, not "grammar" issues or punctuation.
- Ask questions to help the writer generate ideas for clarification and support, and to help the writer extend and complicate her thinking.
- Play devil's advocate: introduce objections or other points of view to help the writer make a more convincing argument.

Get a sense of the whole before formulating your responses.

- If someone is reading a draft aloud, listen to the whole draft before taking notes.
- Listen twice, making notes during the second reading so you can confirm or rethink your first impressions.
- Record your responses in three columns: positive comments, negative comments, and questions.
- If you are reading silently, read the paper through completely, using lines or marginal notes to mark passages you want to look at again or comment on.
- Use a second reading to fill out a peer-response form or decide on the most constructive feedback you might offer.

TABLE 6.1 ● STRATEGIES FOR MANAGING YOUR WRITING PROCESSES (CONTINUED)

Strategies for Peer Response and Revision (Continued)

Tips for Using Peer Feedback to Revise

Let your peer responders know what concerns you about the draft—your goal is to learn how it comes across to readers.

- Ask for feedback in terms of your rhetorical aim.
- Ask your peer responders whether your text accomplished your intended purpose.
- Ask specific questions about passages that you have already identified as problematic.
- Keep an open mind as you listen to peer responses.
- Don't waste time by trying to defend what you've written.
- Expect some contradictory feedback. "Try on" any differing perspectives to determine what in the text is causing them.

Use peer feedback to develop a revision plan.

- Weigh the feedback and decide for yourself where and how to revise.
- What does the feedback tell you about the draft's successes and failures?
- Which responses are the most important to address first?
- Attend to higher-order concerns (focus, organization, development of ideas, logic) before lower-order concerns (sentence-level, grammatical, and mechanical problems).

Strategies for Editing and Polishing the Final Draft

See what's really on the page, not what you hope is there.

- Read your text aloud to yourself or someone else to catch missing words, wrong words, and other kinds of errors.
- Have someone else read your paper back to you. Listen for unclear sentences and awkward wording.
- To slow down your reading, read your paper line by line. Use another sheet of paper to cover the text you have not yet read.
- Keep track of the kinds of errors you habitually make, and be on the lookout for these errors as you proofread.
- Use computerized spelling, grammar, or style aids as only *one* of several steps in your editing process.
- Have a friend or classmate read over your final paper because no matter how careful you are, you may miss some errors.

Strategies for Peer Response and Revision

One of the best ways to see your text differently is through another reader's eyes. Because you know what you meant to write, it is often difficult to see any gaps or confusing points in what is actually on the page. Other readers, not privy to your inner thoughts, can spot these issues much more readily. Peer-response groups allow you to receive feedback from a "live" audience, whether this feedback comes in the form of written or face-to-face oral comments.

The benefits of working in a peer-response group go beyond the insights you gain about your own draft; you also benefit from the experience of offering feedback to others. For one thing, you can learn to recognize and understand various kinds of writing problems by seeing them in someone else's writing. This understanding, with practice, helps you detect those problems when they crop up in your own writing. In addition, offering constructive feedback helps you develop a language for talking about what's working in a text and what's not. This language, in turn, helps you analyze your own writing. Put simply, receiving and giving peer response enables you to achieve the kind of critical distance on your own writing that is so crucial to effective revision.

Perhaps the most frequent complaint we hear from student writers about peer-response groups is that the responders didn't offer any real feedback but instead offered vague, polite comments. To help you make the most of suggestions from peer reviewers and to help you help others with their drafts, Table 6.1 offers a number of suggestions for listening, reading, and responding specifically and productively.

Strategies for Editing and Polishing Your Final Draft

College professors expect final drafts that are carefully edited and proofread. Editing can be difficult, however, because most of us have trouble recognizing the surface errors in our own writing—omitted words, spelling and punctuation errors, wrong or repeated words. We literally fail to see what is on the page; instead, we substitute what we intended to write for what is there. Consequently, you must train yourself to detect and correct errors in sentence structure, word choice, spelling, punctuation, citation conventions, and grammar or usage.

Cautionary advice about computerized proofreading aids: Do not rely solely on grammar and spell checkers to detect the errors in your paper. Spelling checkers, for example, do not detect homonym errors—*its* when you need *it's*—and they don't flag misspellings that turn out to be correctly spelled words that are not what you meant—*cant* for *want*. Similarly, grammar checkers mechanically mark things like passive voice or repeated words that may actually be appropriate in a particular context. For example, the computer highlighted the second *that* in the following sentence: "I believe that that is wrong." But this sentence might be perfectly appropriate in a context where it is clear what the second *that* refers to. Remember that grammar checkers do not actually understand language. To check on word choices, punctuation, grammar, and usage rules as well as citation conventions, keep at hand a recently published handbook. In addition, use an online or paper dictionary to *be sure* a word that you do not often use means what you think it does. Researchers are finding that this kind of error is becoming more frequent. Thus, avoid embarrassment by *never* using a word you find through a thesaurus unless you first double-check its meaning in a separate dictionary.

Finally, because grammar software can flag so many items that don't really need your attention, if you are going to use it, we strongly advise you to wait until you have an almost final draft before you do so. Table 6.1 offers additional tips for focusing on specifics as you polish your final drafts.

Integrating Material from Readings into Your Writing

The effective use of sources in your papers will enable you to position your ideas in relation to those of others and will establish your credibility as an informed writer. Success in this aspect of your writing will be measured by your ability to incorporate the words and ideas of others judiciously (keeping readers' attention on *your* points), smoothly (using clear, grammatically correct sentences), and correctly (representing the points and language of your sources without distortion). Our detailed advice for accomplishing this is summarized with a list of "Do's and Don'ts" in Table 6.2 on page 130. Because each technique serves a useful and distinct purpose, you should become adept at all three so that you can choose the one that best suits a specific purpose within a paper. How you use sources in your texts should result from careful rhetorical choices.

Using Summary

Probably the most common way of incorporating a source into your own writing is through **summary.** As we described in Chapter 3, the reason for summarizing all or part of another writer's text is to present in your own words a condensed version of that writer's points in a way that connects to your own ongoing discussion.

It is best to introduce a summary of others' work with a phrase that alerts the reader to the fact that what follows comes from an outside source, and you must provide an accurate reference that pinpoints where others can find that source. Summarizing is an especially effective rhetorical strategy in the following situations:

- When the source directly supports your thesis, presents ideas you will analyze, or offers a position you wish to argue against
- When the source offers important background information for your ideas

TABLE 6.2 • DO'S AND DON'TS WITH SUMMARIES, PARAPHRASES, AND QUOTATION	
When You Summarize — **Do**	**Don't**
• Make your summary as concise as possible • Represent your source's meaning accurately and fairly	• Distract readers by including points not directly relevant to your purpose
When You Paraphrase — **Do**	**Don't**
• Paraphrase only what you need to develop your points • Be sure you understand the language you are paraphrasing • Recast sentences to create a genuine paraphrase	• Merely change a few words • Distort the original's meaning or intention
When You Quote — **Do**	**Don't**
• Keep the actual quotation as short as possible • Fit the quotation naturally into your own sentence structure • Verify the absolute accuracy of the quotation	• Use quotes as a shortcut around difficult ideas • Distract readers with long quotes
With All Three Techniques	
• Link your text to your sources with clear attributive tags and appropriate citations. • Represent the source fairly and accurately.	

- When you need to provide readers with an overview of a source's whole argument before analyzing particular ideas from it
- When you want to condense and clarify information from a source

The length of your summary will depend on its location and function in your paper. Your goals for your paper will dictate how much of a source you need to summarize. Consider what you want the summary to *do* to move your own points forward. (See pp. 59–64 in Chapter 3 for more details about preparing summaries. You may also want to consult the discussion of the differences between what texts *do* and *say* on pp. 56–58.)

To illustrate how length can vary with purpose, let's examine two summaries of different lengths in Abby's rhetorical analysis of Atul Gawande's op-ed argument, "A Lifesaving Checklist." (Abby's paper, "A Surprising Checklist," is located at the end of Chapter 4, pp. 94–97.) Abby sets the context for her analysis essay with a very brief summary in her opening sentence. Notice how Abby's nutshell version of Gawande's piece echoes her own title theme of "surprise."

SUMMARY EXAMPLE 1

For many *New York Times* readers, it must have been somewhat surprising to encounter Atul Gawande's December 30, 2007, op-ed article criticizing a little known U.S. government office for endangering lives when it ordered a halt to research on the effectiveness of a medical checklist.

In the second example, Abby uses a longer, detailed summary of Gawande's final paragraph to comment on how his reasoning unfolds overall. She includes brief quotes for further illustration.

SUMMARY EXAMPLE 2

Gawande suggests, but never quite says exactly, that stopping the research on the checklist's usefulness violates scientific ethics. In his final paragraph, he almost says it when he asserts that the OHRP authorities are "in danger of putting ethics bureaucracy in the way of actual ethical medical care" (par. 11). His next assertions are even more direct. First, he calls for the research to continue "unencumbered." Then, in his final sentence, he says that if the agency won't allow this to happen, "Congress will have to" (par. 11). It sounds almost like a threat of punishment.

Cautionary advice: We offer two cautions about writing summaries. First, you should summarize only the points that are essential to your purpose. Summaries that are too long or that cover too many points will distract readers from the main flow of your text. Second, make sure that your summary fairly and accurately represents the original text's meaning. Be on guard against distorting the original to make it fit your argument.

Here's the ultimate take-away about a good summary: Ask yourself whether the original author would consider your summary to be fair and accurate.

Using Paraphrase

Unlike a summary, in which you condense the original text's ideas, a **paraphrase** restates in your own words the entirety of the original passage's point. Because paraphrases follow the original wording closely, you must cite the source by

---

BOX 6.1 GUIDELINES FOR EFFECTIVE PARAPHRASE

☐ Avoid mirroring the sentence structure or organization of the original.
☐ Simplify complex ideas by pulling them apart and explaining each smaller component of the larger idea.
☐ Use synonyms for key words in the original and replace unfamiliar or technical vocabulary with more familiar terms.
☐ As a check, try paraphrasing the passage twice, the second time paraphrasing your own paraphrase; then compare your second paraphrase with the original to make sure that you have sufficiently recast it into your own language.

---

page number, if one is available. Often, paraphrases are as long as or even longer than the original, so it is best to paraphrase only short passages.

Paraphrasing is a particularly valuable rhetorical strategy in the following situations:

- When you want to emphasize especially significant ideas by retaining all of the points or details from the original
- When you want to clarify ideas that are complex or language that is dense, technical, or hard to understand

Because paraphrase involves closely re-presenting the original text, you must take care not to give the impression that these are your ideas. Refer to the source at the beginning of the paraphrase. Putting someone else's ideas into your own words does not make these ideas your own. To paraphrase effectively and ethically, you must translate the writer's wording entirely into your own words and acknowledge the source with an attributive tag and a citation. In the guidelines Box 6.1 above, we recommend paraphrasing twice: once from the source, then again from your own paraphrase.

To illustrate the process and rhetorical effects of paraphrasing, we invite you to consider the parallels and variations between a passage from Jack's paper about multiple perspectives on corn-based ethanol, located at the end of this chapter (pp. 145–152), and one of his sources.

DIALOG FROM THE ONLINE TRANSCRIPT OF A *NEWSHOUR* VIDEO[1]

[IOWA] SEN. TOM HARKIN: You're going to see a lot of marginal land that's not suitable for row crop production, because it's hilly, or it's not very productive for corn or soybeans, things like that, but it can be very productive for grasses,

---

[1]Heidi Cullen, "In Iowa, Questions Arise About the Impact of Ethanol Production." *Online NewsHour*. PBS, 28 Jan. 2009. Web.

like miscanthus, or switchgrass, and you can use that to make the cellulose ethanol.

HEIDI CULLEN: And using such land for growing fuel can help with the carbon dioxide problem, for in turning these kinds of plant materials into ethanol, you eliminate the need to use land suitable for food, feed for animals, and fiber for paper.

Jack recognized this exchange as important to the issue of "food-versus-fuel" land use, but knew that trying to introduce Senator Harkin and quote him would take up too much space and throw off his organizational strategy. The information about where these crops could be grown was more important than the fact that Senator Harkin provided the information. So Jack decided to paraphrase and cite the Cullen video, knowing that anyone who wanted to follow up could find more detail simply by searching in the transcript for "switchgrass." Notice that he has been able to boil down the points to a concise paraphrase and thus use this paraphrase to elaborate on the point that moves his paper from his third major issue to his fourth.

JACK'S PARAPHRASE

For people concerned about the fourth issue, using food crop acreage to grow fuel crops, the prospect of cellulosic ethanol offers great hope. For one thing, using products other than corn kernels for ethanol production has the advantage that many of these alternative crops, such as switchgrass (ordinarily grown for hay), can be grown on "marginal" or hilly land where food crops cannot be grown (Cullen).

Cautionary advice: Paraphrasing difficult ideas or dense passages is a good way not only to help your readers understand material but also to demonstrate your own understanding of it. However, recasting scholarly or technical language can be difficult. We offer advice on three points. (1) Take care to avoid the problem of inadequate paraphrase. If your paraphrase is too close to the original wording, you may open yourself to a charge of plagiarism. (2) To avoid the potential problem of inaccurate presentation, be sure you fully understand any passage you are paraphrasing. One valuable technique is to imagine how you would convey the gist of the source's point conversationally. If you can't move beyond the words of the original, it's likely that you need to obtain a better understanding of the ideas before you use them in your paper. Quoting is not the way to solve this problem. In fact, quoting an entire passage can actually make matters worse. Long quotations suggest that you find the original points so daunting that you cannot put them into your own words. (3) As with summary, be concise: Paraphrase from the original only what you need to develop your points in detail. A long paraphrase can draw so much attention to itself that it distracts the reader. Instead, keep readers focused on your ideas about how the source material fits your points.

Using Direct Quotation

Direct quotation inserts the words of someone else into your own text. Whenever you use another writer's exact wording, you must mark the beginning and end of the passage with quotation marks and provide as precise a reference to the original source as possible. Used selectively and sparingly, quotations strengthen your credibility by showing that you have consulted appropriate authorities on a particular subject. However, quoting too frequently or using unnecessarily long quotations can actually undermine your credibility. Overreliance on direct quotations weakens your authority and suggests that you have no ideas of your own to contribute to the conversation.

Direct quotations are most effective in enhancing your credibility in the following situations:

- When the language of the source is vivid, distinctive, or memorable
- When the quotation directly supports a key point in your paper
- When the person quoted is such a well-known authority on the matter that even a few well-chosen words will carry considerable weight

To illustrate the value of keeping quotations short, we present two versions of a passage from Jack's ethanol paper. In his first draft, Jack wanted to develop his first major point, that production of corn ethanol uses extensive petroleum resources, by including an exchange from an online discussion. In a draft, he tried out the long quotation in the following passage.

INEFFECTIVE LONG QUOTATION FROM JACK'S FIRST DRAFT

Responding to a questioner who asked whether "the EROEI [energy return on energy investment] on corn ethanol [is] such that it is a feasible candidate to replace petroleum for some of our energy needs," Robert P. Anex, associate director of the Office of Biorenewables Programs at Iowa State University, said, "The energy return on energy investment (EROEI) of corn grain ethanol is positive (the 'ethanol fuel energy out to fossil energy in' ratio is about 1.3), but ethanol is not the goal of a biofuels program. The goals are things like enhanced national security, improved environmental quality, and local economic development. For example, [a 2006 article published in *Science*] *Farrell* et al., found that corn grain ethanol does much better at displacing petroleum use than at displacing fossil energy but really excels at reducing greenhouse gas emissions. Ultimately, we cannot achieve our goals through corn grain ethanol alone, but corn ethanol has developed a biofuel market and has thereby made possible corporate investment in cellulosic ethanol that can have a much larger positive impact on the multiple goals associated with biofuels development" (Brainard).[2]

As you can see, by quoting the dialog, especially with the necessary bracketed explanations, Jack risked losing control of his paper. He recognized Anex's response as highly important to his ultimate points—here was an expert indicating both the usefulness and limits of corn ethanol in the evolving story of clean biofuels. But the phrasing was unique to the context of the discussion, and, as he recognized, it was too long to quote. He had to decide which was the most important of Anex's several points, then help his readers understand that point and its importance. Here is Jack's revision, which cuts the original version (184 words) by two-thirds, to 62 words. More important still is that the way in which he establishes context for the quote within his own paper prevents his source from taking over the paragraph.

JACK'S REVISED USE OF QUOTATION

A University of Iowa scientist explains away the problem of corn ethanol's resource intensity as "just a step along the way" (Brainard). In a Web discussion sponsored by the *Chronicle of Higher Education*, Robert P. Anex, associate director of the Office of Biorenewables Programs at Iowa State, said the real goals are "enhanced national security, improved environmental quality, and local economic development."[3]

The guidelines in Box 6.2 on page 136 will help you quote accurately and effectively.

Cautionary advice: First, not only is absolute accuracy in quotations important ethically, but any inaccuracies will undermine your credibility. Second, be sure that you are not quoting someone out of context. Doing so is a surprisingly common mistake because complex texts or unfamiliar subject matter can make it difficult to recognize changes in tone or references to opposing views. Be sure that the way you use a quotation does not misconstrue or misinterpret its original meaning.

● FOR WRITING AND DISCUSSION

One way to develop skill at incorporating the ideas of others into your own papers is to see how other writers do it. To try this out, track the use of direct quotations in Jack's paper at the end of this chapter.

---

[2]Jeffrey Brainard, "The Race to Harvest Energy." *Chronicle of Higher Education: Live Discussions.* Chronicle of Higher Education, 24 Apr. 2007. Web. 30 Mar. 2009. Transcript.

[3]Jack does not need to include a parenthetical cite after the second sentence in which he quotes Anex because it can only be understood as from the same original passage. Providing the parenthetical citation after the first quote-containing sentence lets the reader know the source right away.

BOX 6.2 GUIDELINES FOR USING DIRECT QUOTATIONS EFFECTIVELY

☐ Favor short quotations. Use long quotations only rarely because they will distract from the focus of your own discussion.

☐ Whenever possible, instead of quoting whole sentences, work quotations of key phrases into your own sentences.

☐ Make sure you are absolutely accurate in the wording of direct quotations.

☐ Punctuate your quotations exactly as in the original.

☐ If you must use a longer quotation, instead of using quotation marks, set the material off from the text using block indentation. In MLA format, quotations longer than four typed lines start on a new line, are indented a full inch, and are double-spaced.

☐ Make sure you represent the original source fairly and accurately.

☐ Make sure you fully understand the ideas that you quote directly. Although the words in a quotation may sound impressive, if you cannot explain them and connect them with your own ideas, incorporating the quotation will detract from your credibility instead of enhancing it.

☐ As part of your proofreading routine, compare all quoted material to the original passage and make any needed adjustments, no matter how small.

ON YOUR OWN

Note all the places where Jack uses direct quotations, and describe how each quotation is used—what it *does*. Find places, for example, where he uses sources to support or illustrate one of his points, to represent an opinion he admires, to increase his credibility, or to capture vivid or distinctive language from a source. Some of his direct quotations may serve more than one function.

WITH YOUR CLASSMATES

Compare your lists and descriptions. Are there differences or disagreements about how a particular direct quotation is being used? How effectively does Jack use quotations? Are there any quotations that might have been eliminated or shortened? Are there any places where you think his paper might have been strengthened by the use of a direct quotation where there isn't one?

Avoiding Plagiarism

Whether you are summarizing, paraphrasing, or quoting, you must give credit to others' words and ideas by using a recognized system for referring readers to your sources. One such system is the MLA's, explained later in this chapter and in the appendix. The MLA system, widely used in undergraduate classes, uses short in-text citations that refer to a full list of sources at the end of the paper.

You must acknowledge borrowed ideas and information. All directly quoted language must be marked as such with quotation marks or appropriately indented formatting. Even if you are quoting only a short phrase from the original source, quotation marks are essential. Omission of either the quotation marks or the reference information has the effect of creating a text that presents someone else's words or ideas as if they were your own. In that case, you are committing **plagiarism**, a serious form of academic misconduct in which a writer takes material from someone else's work and fraudulently presents it as if it were the writer's own ideas and wording, either intentionally or unintentionally.

The three most common forms of plagiarism are the following:

- Failure to use quotation marks to indicate borrowed language
- Failure to acknowledge borrowed ideas and information
- Failure to change the language of the source text sufficiently in a paraphrase

Student writers sometimes have problems managing the details of quotations because they neglect to take careful notes that clearly mark all directly quoted material. During their revision processes, inexperienced writers sometimes lose track of which sentences and phrases are directly quoted. To avoid such problems and symptoms of potential plagiarism, make sure you take scrupulous care to mark all directly quoted language and its source in your notes and drafts. **Write down all relevant bibliographic information even before you begin reading and taking notes.** This is especially important if you are "taking notes" by copying and pasting material from an electronic source into a notes file. Some writers use color highlighting for this process, or put directly quoted language in a different font so that, as they move passages around during drafting and revision, they can keep track of which words are directly quoted even if the quotation marks disappear when changes are made. Other writers keep full original quotations at the end of the paper file or in a separate electronic file so that they can check for accuracy and proper citation as part of their final preparations before submission.

You must acknowledge borrowed ideas and information through appropriate citation. That is, all ideas and information that are not your own—including statistics—require citation through attributive tags, internal citation, and the list of sources at the end of the paper. The only exception is common knowledge. Common knowledge, as the phrase suggests, refers to information and knowledge that is widely known. (For example: George Washington was the first U.S. president, or thunderstorms are more likely in hot weather.) You can verify that certain information is common knowledge by consulting general information sources such as encyclopedias. If you are in doubt about whether something is common knowledge, or if you are concerned that your readers might credit an idea to you that is not yours, refer to and cite the source.

Perhaps the most difficult aspect of incorporating sources in a way that avoids plagiarism is sufficiently rewording the language of a source when you paraphrase. (This is why we recommend paraphrasing source material twice.) As we noted in the section on paraphrase, using the same sentence pattern as the original source and changing only a few words does not create an acceptable paraphrase, even if the writer includes a reference to the source. In the following examples, compare the acceptable and unacceptable paraphrases with the original passage from the *Consumer Reports* article "The Ethanol Myth," a major source for Jack's paper.

ORIGINAL PASSAGE FROM SOURCE

The FFV surge is being motivated by generous fuel-economy credits that automakers get for every FFV they build, even if it never runs on E85. This allows them to pump out more gas-guzzling large SUVs and pickups, which is resulting in the consumption of many times more gallons of gasoline than E85 now replaces.[4]

UNACCEPTABLE PARAPHRASE—TOO CLOSE TO THE ORIGINAL SYNTAX AND WORD CHOICES

The increase in FFV production is caused by big fuel-economy credits that automakers get for every FFV, which are gas-guzzling large SUVs and pickups, which results in consuming many more gallons of gasoline than E85 replaces ("Ethanol Myth" 16).

ACCEPTABLE PARAPHRASE

...the article strongly criticizes federal tax breaks for FFV manufacturers, arguing that the tax breaks have encouraged automakers to overproduce FFVs, most of which happen to be large, inefficient SUVs and pickups. Because of the shortage of E85 gas stations, FFVs run most of the time on regular gasoline, making advertisements about their being innovative "an empty promise," the writers say (16). The result, according to *CR*, is "the consumption of many times more gallons of gasoline than E85 now replaces" (16).

Jack's revision serves as a model of what to do when paraphrasing is difficult:

1. He added phrasing that links the key point to his source's overall point.
2. He combined the points in the passage that he had trouble paraphrasing with relevant information elsewhere in the source, including direct quotes of two powerful phrases.

---

[4]"The Ethanol Myth." *Consumer Reports* Oct. 2006: 15–19. *EbscoHost.* Web. 3 Apr. 2009.

By following the guidelines we present for quoting and paraphrasing, you can avoid plagiarism. We close this section by passing along a final bit of advice: when you are incorporating materials from outside sources, write with your eyes on your own text, not on your source's sentences.[5] Your unfolding text should come from your mind, not someone else's text.

Using Attributive Tags to Frame Sources Rhetorically

All three of the techniques we have described for incorporating source material—summary, paraphrase, and quotation—work best with **attributive tags**. These are short phrases or tags that connect or attribute material to its source, for example, "Ariel Jones says …" or "According to Ariel Jones…." In the process of acknowledging the source, the tags can also enhance the rhetorical effect of your text by giving readers valuable information about the credibility of your sources, shaping your readers' response to it, and demonstrating that you, not your sources, are in charge. The following discussion explains how these phrases can do all this.[6] Specific guidelines for composing tags are provided in Box 6.3.

1. Attributive tags help readers distinguish your sentences and ideas from those in your sources (whether summarized, paraphrased, or quoted). In fact, a lack of attributive tags is often symptomatic of the passive writing we have been warning against. As illustration, let's consider the difference between two versions of a sentence from Jack's paper.

CONFUSION CAUSED BY LACK OF ATTRIBUTIVE TAG

The ethanol boom has led farmers to give up subsidies that the Conservation Reserve Program had previously paid them to keep land out of production. "When this land is planted with corn, all of the carbon that's stored in these prairie grasses and in these trees is released back into the atmosphere" (Cullen).

In the above passage, the reader expects a citation for the information in the first sentence. The reader is likely to be confused, therefore, when the next sentence opens with a quotation, signaling that another voice has entered the text. The reader doesn't know where the quoted material comes from and may not

---

[5]This advice comes from *The Craft of Research* by Wayne Booth, Gregory Colomb, and Joseph Williams, who say, "If your eyes are on your source at the same moment your fingers are flying across the keyboard, you risk doing something that weeks, months, even years later could result in your public humiliation" (Chicago: U Chicago P, 1995), 170. Print.

[6]We are grateful to freelance writer Robert McGuire, formerly a writing instructor at Marquette University, for his valuable insights and advice about attributive tags.

BOX 6.3 GUIDELINES FOR USING ATTRIBUTIVE TAGS EFFECTIVELY

☐ Make the tag part of your own sentence.

☐ The first time you bring in a particular source, put the tag before the quotation or summary so that readers will have the background they need when they reach the borrowed source material.

☐ Vary the format and vocabulary of your tags. You want to avoid a long string of phrases that repeat "according to" or "he says."

☐ Provide just enough background to help readers understand the significance of the material you are bringing in, not everything there is to say about the source.

☐ Base your decisions about attributive tags on what you are confident readers will recognize and what will help them understand the relevance of the source you are using. For example, *Time* is a well-known magazine and the *Journal of Urban History* has a self-explanatory title, so using those titles in a tag would probably provide more context than an author's name would. However, stating that an article appeared in a journal with an ambiguous title—we are aware of at least three periodicals named *Dialogue*, for example—would probably be pointless without further explanation. In many cases, rather than use space explaining the audience for and purpose of the journal, it would be preferable to supply a brief context-setting phrase about the author's background or about how the material you are using fits the larger published conversation.

---

recall the name cited at the end from earlier in the paper. If curious, one would have to go to the works cited list.

But the following revised version is much better because the attributive tag in the introductory prepositional phrase refers back to the source ("Cullen") identified earlier in the paragraph. Now the reader knows that Cullen is the source for the information in the first sentence and is also the person quoted in the second sentence:

SENTENCE REVISED WITH ATTRIBUTIVE TAG

As Cullen explains in her video, the ethanol boom has led farmers to give up subsidies that the federal government had previously paid them in order to preserve land by keeping it out of production. "When this land is planted with corn," she notes, "all of the carbon that's stored in these prairie grasses and in these trees is released back into the atmosphere."

2. Attributive tags enhance your credibility by showing readers that you are careful with source materials and remain in charge of the paper. You are the one lining up and tying together source materials to fit your purposes for writing.

3. Attributive tags can enhance your text's credibility by indicating the credentials or reputation of an expert you are using as a source. For example, you might say "high school teacher Sam Delaney," "Molly Smith, an avid fan of romance literature," or "Josephine DeLoria, a controversial defense lawyer." Sometimes, credentials will convey more information than a name will: "the Justice Department's main espionage prosecutor for over twenty years."

4. Attributive tags provide a quick method of showing readers the published context of your source material. This context will help you show how the text you are writing fits within a published conversation. Here are some examples: "In her review of Victoria M. Johnson's book, Martha Smith argues…," "Kim Ochimuru, in an article detailing the results of the Harvard study, contends… ," or "A letter to the editor objecting to the paper's editorial stance outlines the following complaint."

5. Attributive tags give you the opportunity to shape readers' responses to the material you are presenting. The verb you choose to describe the source's influence is important because it will suggest your attitude toward the source. Some verbs suggest that you agree with the source; others suggest doubt about what the source says. For example, the first of the following examples conveys the writer's positive attitude toward the source material being introduced; the second conveys a skeptical attitude, leading the reader to expect that the writer will counter the source's point:

A July 2009 *Time* magazine article verifies this claim.

Some literary critics claim that the books depend too much on magic.

Attributive tags work best near the beginning of a sentence, but can be placed after other introductory phrases at any natural break. Here are some examples of tags placed at different points in sentences:

Published as a *Newsweek* online exclusive, Kliff's article…

The result of the automakers' tax breaks and the difficulty of finding E85 fuel, *Consumer Reports* says, is…

The Union of Concerned Scientists (UCS) notes, for example,…

Your first attributive tag about a source is likely to be longer than subsequent ones, as illustrated by these contrasting examples from Jack's paper:

As reporter Heidi Cullen explains in a PBS *NewsHour* video,…

As Cullen explains in her video…

Here's the explanation that an Iowa farmer gave Cullen…

In some instances, an author's name may not be as interesting or important to your readers as the place where an article appeared. For example, the reference to the *NewsHour* in the first example tells readers much more than Cullen's name alone would have, either in the sentence or in the parenthetical citation. The same kind of informativeness comes from the periodical title in the following example:

> A July 2000 *Time* magazine article verifies this claim and reports that over 50% of all paperbacks sold in the United States each year are romance novels (Gray and Sachs 76).

As the preceding examples illustrate, attributive tags can offer a variety of information in accordance with a writer's purpose and sense of the intended audience's background knowledge. The possibilities range from facts that appear in citations (e.g., author's name, work's title, publisher, or date) to supplementary details about the author (e.g., credentials or purpose) or about the work (e.g., its context or reputation since publication). Of course, if you used all this information in one tag, the sentence would have hardly any room left for your own ideas. You do not want to overwhelm your readers with details that do not immediately convey significance. Readers can always find complete titles and publication information on your works cited list. If you decide readers need a lot of background, you may want to provide it in a separate sentence, as Jack does when he introduces the *Consumer Reports* article that he will refer back to frequently in his paper:

> A careful, consumer-focused exploration of both the negatives and positives of corn ethanol as fuel was published by *Consumer Reports* (*CR*) in 2006, during the war in Iraq, a time when alternative fuels and vehicles that could use them were being widely discussed. This magazine is known as a watchdog, a guide to help consumers make wise purchases, especially on big budget items such as automobiles. The article focuses primarily on road tests of flex fuel vehicles (FFVs)....

Using Parenthetical Citations

Clear, accurate **citations** of outside sources are an essential element of academic writing. Designed to help readers locate source materials, citations present a formalized statement of a work's author, title, publication date, publisher, medium of publication, and exact location—that is, page numbers and/or an Internet address. As we explained in the section on avoiding plagiarism, citations are required for statistics, quotations, paraphrases, and summaries of other writers' work and ideas—any information that is not common knowledge.

Although discussions of citations tend to focus on their formal properties, it is important to recognize that they have rhetorical functions as well. Citations enhance your own credibility because they reveal the quality of the sources you have used. By positioning your ideas within a published conversation, they help guide your reader's response to your text. When handled well, they enhance a text's readability as well as your own credentials as an academic writer.

Understanding Academic Citation Conventions[7]

All academic disciplines require that you cite sources, but different disciplines use different formats, known as **citation conventions.** These conventions specify particular formats for presenting information that refers readers to a source. In this book, we discuss the Modern Language Association (MLA) format, used widely in the humanities. The MLA system, updated in 2009, relies on brief **in-text** or **parenthetical citations** in the body of the paper to signal that material has come from an outside source. The full citation for that source is found readily via an alphabetical list of authors' last names from all citations in the paper placed at the paper's end and entitled "Works Cited." These complete citations convey two important pieces of information to readers: (1) what kinds of materials the writer used as a basis for the current text, and (2) exactly where the material used in the paper can be found.

In-text citations are placed in parentheses to minimize the intrusion of bibliographic information on the reading experience. If a writer has followed citation conventions carefully, readers hardly notice the cites as they read but can return to use them to find additional information efficiently. Here's an example from Jack's paper.

MLA IN-TEXT CITATION

...called for expansion of research on emissions "to include a broad array of environmental quality dimensions" (Hill et al. 1081).

Authors' names inside the parentheses tell readers where to find the full citation of the work on the alphabetized works cited list at the end of the paper.

CORRESPONDING FULL CITATION ON MLA WORKS CITED LIST

Hill, Jason, et al. "Climate Change and Health Costs of Air Emissions from Biofuels and Gasoline." *Proceedings of the National Academy of Science* 106.6 (2009): 1077–1082. *PubMed Central.* Web. 6 Apr. 2009.

The specific page number in the parenthetical in-text citation allows the reader to pinpoint the cited material.

---

[7]Our discussion here and in the appendix is based on the *MLA Handbook for Writers of Research Papers*, 7th ed. (New York: MLA, 2009). Print.

Before we go any further, we want to assure you that the details of citation conventions are not something to memorize. Scholars regularly consult models and guidelines such as those in this chapter and the appendix. You should do the same.

The content of citations communicates important information about the context and purpose of sources, and thus about the reliability and authority of the source materials. When you read scholarly articles in specialized courses for your major, you will discover that citations are also an invaluable source of information about where you can find additional resources for research projects.

In some courses, particularly history, instead of in-text citations you may be asked to use footnotes that follow the format laid out in the *Chicago Manual of Style* (also called Turabian format, after the author whose handbooks popularized it). Furthermore, professors in the social sciences might ask you to follow specialized conventions for their discipline, particularly the parenthetical author-date format of the American Psychological Association. Professors in natural science and technical classes, where it is common to refer repeatedly to many sources, may ask you to use a citation-sequence method for in-text references such as that laid out in the Council of Science (formerly Biology) Editors' *CBE Manual* or a numbering system based on the overall alphabetical order of the sources in a list at the end of the paper. These and other formats are described in many composition handbooks; furthermore, specialized guides are readily available online or at library reference desks.[8] Whenever you are not sure what is expected regarding citations, check with your instructor.

Chapter Summary

In this chapter we offered tips for managing your writing process and discussed the importance of the following:

- Asserting your own authority when you use readings; that is, making your points in your own voice rather than patching together quotes and paraphrases from sources
- Claiming and maintaining your authority as you generate ideas and draft your paper
- Reading and analyzing your own drafts rhetorically so that you attend to both your content ("what") and your methods ("how") as you revise through multiple drafts

We then described when and how to use summary, paraphrase, and direct quotation, and explained that skillful incorporation of source materials into your

---

[8]Online writing centers usually have helpful information that is easy to access. Try the Web sites for the centers at Purdue <http://owl.english.purdue.edu/owl/resource/585/01/> or the University of Wisconsin <http://writing.wisc.edu/Handbook/DocMLA.html>.

own texts enhances your credibility and clarifies how your ideas fit into the larger published conversation about a topic. Throughout the discussion we emphasized the importance of subordinating source materials to your own purposes, ideas, and organization. We stressed the importance of careful note-taking as a means of avoiding even inadvertent plagiarism. The guidelines we provided show how to

- Incorporate brief summaries, paraphrases, and direct quotations into your work
- Avoid plagiarism by using genuine paraphrases, taking careful notes, and attending to the details of bibliographic information
- Use attributive tags to help shape the response you desire from readers
- Provide clear and correct in-text citations using MLA formatting

In the sample student paper that follows, you will find numerous examples of these techniques. The appendix to this book provides details about using MLA format for both parenthetical citations and the full citations used in lists of works cited, including model citations for many types of materials you will be likely to use in your own papers.

Incorporating Reading into Writing: An Example in MLA Format

Here is Jack's analysis of multiple perspectives on corn ethanol, written in response to the assignment at the beginning of Chapter 5 (p. 103).

1

Arguing on the Basis of Wishful Thinking:
An Analysis of Multiple Perspectives
on Corn-Based Ethanol

Title echoes assignment.

Where I'm from in Iowa, just about everything is about corn: growing it, harvesting it, selling it, driving it. Driving it? Yes. Many Iowans think that corn-based ethanol is the best thing since gasoline; they consider it the answer to America's worries over energy security because it will make us less reliant on imported oil. Other people think that corn-based ethanol is a terrible thing, that increasing its production is stealing land otherwise used for growing food with the result of not only raising food prices around the world but destroying rain forests (because of trees cut down for farmland), which in turn

Intro paragraph with personal flavor lays out extreme attitudes re subject matter.

increases the rate of global warming. These extreme attitudes are just two of many varying perspectives about the
extent to which corn-based ethanol either offers hope for
cleaner, safer energy along a path that will reduce global
warming or threatens economic destruction for farmers
and increases the threat of climate change.

2   Although the discussion about ethanol, specifically
ethanol distilled from corn, is often framed by both the
press and activists as a "food v. fuel debate," it is far
more complex than over-simplified headlines or protest
banners suggest. The real problem is that nobody has
enough information yet to know the best way to produce
ethanol—from corn or from some other plant crop. "Clean
energy" seems like a good idea, but so far, nobody has
demonstrated that ethanol promises a good future for any
of us, for farmers who just want to make a good living, or
for consumers who just want to drive a safe, economical
car without feeling guilty about harming the environment.

3   Of course, farmers and consumers alike have to make
decisions before they know what the outcomes will be.
They take a risk and make a choice, hoping that oil prices
and the overall economy will work out for that choice to
be a good one. But people who claim to be certain about
the wisdom of investing in ethanol, or in cars fueled by
it, are basing their arguments primarily on hope and
wishful thinking. We won't know the answers for many
years to come.

4   Important recent news about corn-based ethanol is
that as of January 1, 2012, Congress ended tax credits
for companies that blend ethanol into gasoline. What is
surprising about this news is that, according to *New York
Times* reporter Robert Pear, the gasoline refiners (the big
users of the ethanol) are not worried about it. In
fact, Pear reported, "Ethanol proponents eventually
accepted expiration of the tax credit without putting up a
big fight." To explain this phenomenon, a spokesman for
the Renewable Fuels Association (RFA) told Pear that

Intro closes with implicit promise of what is to come, providing rationale for analysis paper. Purely descriptive sentence is not a thesis.

Thesis statement changes focus of the issue away from "food v. fuel"—this is the point that paper will develop.

Third paragraph elaborates on and restates the thesis, clarifying what to expect in paper.

First of two paragraphs relating important background facts.

Detailed tags provide valuable details about background of material cited—journalist and spokesman for RFA (supports increased ethanol production).

"The marketplace has evolved. The tax incentive is less necessary now than it was just two years ago. Ethanol is 10 percent of the nation's gasoline supply." He expects both the price of corn and the amount of ethanol produced in the coming year to be unchanged—good news for both farmers and the ethanol industry.

Many sources report that corn ethanol production has been growing in recent years. In 2011, 40% of the U.S. corn crop was used for ethanol, a larger percentage than went to livestock feed, according to National Public Radio's Dustin Dwyer. He points out that even though the tax break has gone away, government policies still mandate that gas refineries blend corn ethanol into gasoline, a huge support for the industry. The current standard for the blend is 10% ethanol, but 15% is a major goal for the ethanol industry, which also promotes 85% ethanol fuel for flex-fuel engines. (The 10% ethanol, 90% gasoline mix is generally recognized as reducing emissions without a significant decrease in power or miles per gallon.)

Use of the 15% fuel blend, known as E15, was authorized by the Environmental Protection Agency for use in vehicles made since 2001, but it is highly controversial because of decreases in power and efficiency as well as reported damage to small engines such as those on chainsaws and lawn mowers. According to the *DesMoines Register*, research by a group called the Coordinating Research Council (CRC) showed that the higher blend could also damage car engines (Piller). The CRC is run by a coalition of the Petroleum Institute and an international group of automakers. Unstated is the likely fact that to accommodate E15, car engines would need to be redesigned. The CRC's claims were denounced within the article by a spokesman from the Iowa RFA, who called the research "just bad science" (Piller).

5

No parenthetical citations needed in the summary and quotations from Pear's article because his name is in sentence and no page numbers available on Web.

Fifth paragraph broadens context and provides definitions.

6

Controversy is introduced and documented.

Newspaper's title used in sentence because city's name has more significance than author's name. Citation with author's name is essential connection to works cited page.

New paragraph
for perspective
from environ-
mentalists.

7   Environmentalists are not enthusiastic about the increased use of corn ethanol in gasoline, either, but for
different reasons. Friends of the Earth celebrated the
end of the ethanol tax subsidy with a blog posting that
said, "Good riddance to a terrible policy that supported
corporate polluters at the expense of environmental and
social sustainability" (Rosenoer). According to the blogger, this subsidy, which had been in place since 1979,
had "wreaked havoc on our natural resources, raised food
prices, increased world hunger, and diverted federal fund-
ing from truly renewable energy technologies like wind,
solar, and electric vehicles" (Rosenoer).

Jack turns to
outside analysts
for in-depth
background.

Citation uses
short title to
connect with
works cited.

8   As the "Times Topics" section of the *New York Times*
explains, the basic problem is that while ethanol is a
clean-burning fuel, "ethanol production consumes pro-
digious quantities of natural gas, diesel fuel and other
inputs that lead to carbon dioxide emissions" ("Ethanol").
A careful, consumer-focused exploration of both the nega-
tives and positives of corn ethanol as fuel was published
by *Consumer Reports* (*CR*) in 2006, during the war in
Iraq, a time when alternative fuels and vehicles that could
use them were being widely discussed. This magazine is
known as a watchdog, a guide to help consumers make
wise purchases, especially on big budget items such as
automobiles. The article focuses primarily on road tests of
flex fuel vehicles (FFVs) that can run on either gasoline
or E85, a fuel that is 85% ethanol and 15% gasoline. The
article's title, "The Ethanol Myth," announces right away
that *CR* considers FFVs not to be particularly good choices
both because very few gas stations supply E85 and because vehicles operating on E85 "get cleaner emissions
but poorer fuel economy" (15).

Next two para-
graphs provide
extended
summary and
response re-
garding *CR*
article.

9   The *CR* writers want to debunk the myth that ethanol
will somehow become the answer to U.S. energy independence. After reporting their test results, the article
strongly criticizes federal tax breaks for FFV manufacturers, arguing that the tax breaks have encouraged

automakers to overproduce FFVs, most of which happen to be large, inefficient SUVs and pickups. Because there is a shortage of E85 gas stations, FFVs run most of the time on regular gasoline, making advertisements about their being innovative "an empty promise," the writers say (16). The result, according to *CR*, is "the consumption of many times more gallons of gasoline than E85 now replaces" (16). Consumers Union, the organization that publishes *CR*, proposes that federal funds instead be used to stimulate the development of cars that are more fuel efficient overall.

The *CR* article supplies excellent background about   10 the many issues that make ethanol production such a hot topic. Reading it might turn someone who was shopping for an FFV into a skeptic about ethanol as automobile fuel. Four major issues mentioned in the article have come up over and over in discussions about ethanol published since the *CR* article first came out. They include (1) the great amount of petroleum-based resources that are used in the production and transport of ethanol, (2) the question of whether corn ethanol actually adds to or reduces the balance of greenhouse gases in comparison to either gasoline or ethanol from sources other than corn kernels, (3) the need to develop ethanol from other crops, such as switch grass, cornstalks, and sugar cane, into what is called cellulosic ethanol, considered more efficient because its production consumes less fossil fuel, and (4) whether it is wise, or dangerous, to devote agricultural land to fuel crops rather than food crops.

Summary's concluding sentence forecasts what follows.

The first issue, the fact that corn ethanol production is highly energy intensive, concerns many people.   11 Petroleum-based resources are used across the life cycle of the product, from fertilizer and pesticides, to mechanical tilling and harvesting, to distillation and then transport to stations where consumers can pump it into their cars. As reporter Heidi Cullen explains in a PBS *News-Hour* video, while 10 gallons of ethanol may look like 10 gallons of

Note Jack's use of transitions.

renewable energy, "when you account for the eight gallons of fossil fuel used to grow, harvest, and convert the crop to ethanol, you end up with only two gallons of green renewable energy." Nonetheless, she goes on to point out, the 20 percent gain does represent "an improvement over gasoline from the standpoint of both energy and greenhouse gas emissions." Another problem comes from the strain of corn production on the land itself. As Cullen explains in her video, the ethanol boom has led many farmers to give up payments from the federal Conservation Reserve Program to keep some of their land out of production. "When this land is planted with corn," she notes, "all of the carbon that's stored in these prairie grasses and in these trees is released back into the atmosphere."

Brief paragraph adds emphasis to the expert opinion countering that in previous paragraph.

12   A University of Iowa scientist explains away the problem of corn ethanol's resource intensity as "just a step along the way" (Brainard). In a Web discussion sponsored by the *Chronicle of Higher Education*, Robert P. Anex, associate director of the Office of Biorenewables Programs at Iowa State, said the real goals are "enhanced national security, improved environmental quality, and local economic development.

Citation names author who wrote up the Web chat with Anex, the expert quoted.

Research reported from another set of experts.

13   The second major issue, the emissions impact of corn ethanol, leads directly to the third, development of cellulosic ethanol from new crops. Researchers at the University of Minnesota have found that cellulosic ethanol can have a greater positive impact than was previously thought and have called for expansion of research on emissions "to include a broad array of environmental quality dimensions" (Hill et al. 1081). They, like *Consumer Reports*, call for conservation, specifically, "improved emissions controls[,] ... increases in fuel efficiency[,] and fuel conservation ... that would reduce the need for increased fuel supplies" (1081). But here's the catch: economical ways of producing cellulosic ethanol have yet to be found.

Paragraph's closing sentence and colloquial tone pave the way for Jack's closing points, which link back to the thesis.

For people concerned about the fourth issue, using   14
food crop acreage to grow fuel crops, the prospect of cellulosic ethanol offers great hope. For one thing, products
such as switchgrass (ordinarily grown for hay) can be
grown on "marginal" or hilly land where food crops cannot be grown (Cullen). Professor Anex from Iowa State
told an online questioner that decisions about "food
v. fuel" are ultimately moral decisions, which, he hopes,
will be based on "the best science possible" (Brainard).

The biofuels story is ever-changing as research contin-   15
ues and the world economic situation fluctuates. It seems
inevitable that the current flow of corn ethanol will ebb
away because, as everyone knows at some level, we do
live in a world of limited resources. *Consumer Reports*
tells us straight out: "Even with the most optimistic es-
timates, ethanol on its own will never be able to provide
Americans with energy independence" (19). It's more
than likely, they go on to say, that "ethanol will be one
in a portfolio of choices" for clean transportation energy.
In the words of one of my favorite TV ads a few years
back, from the oil company Chevron, no less: "The world
is changing. And how we use energy today cannot be how
we'll use it tomorrow. There is no one solution. It's not
simply more oil, more renewables, or being more efficient.
It's all of it."

Let's hope THAT is not wishful thinking.   16

Voices from paragraphs #11 and 12 brought back for Jack's elaboration on *CR* article's fourth point.

Jack again uses a personal tone in concluding commentary, leaning on the *CR* article for authority and bringing in the irony of the oil company's conservation ad before his final comment, which echoes his title.

Works Cited

Brainard, Jeffrey. "The Race to Harvest Energy."
  Chronicle of Higher Education: Live Discussions.
  Chronicle of Higher Education, 24 Apr. 2007. Web.
  30 Mar. 2009. <http://chronicle.com/live/2007/04/
  anex>. Transcript.

Chevron Corporation. "Tomorrow." *Chevron Television
  and Print Advertising.* You Tube, n.d. Web. 10 June
  2012. <http://www.youtube.com/watch?v=CSkScYdl
  puw>.

Works cited list would start on new page in actual paper.

List continues the double-spacing in the paper and is formatted with hanging indents.

"n.d." = "no date"

Cullen, Heidi. "In Iowa, Questions Arise About the
   Impact of Ethanol Production." *Online NewsHour*. PBS,
   28 Jan. 2009. Web. 3 July 2012. <http://www.pbs.org/
   newshour/bb/environment/jan-june09/
   mixedyield_01-28.html>. Transcript.

Dwyer, Dustin. "After Backlash, Ethanol Industry Is
   Thriving." *Morning Edition*. National Public Radio, 26
   Apr. 2012. Web. 28 May 2012. <http://www.npr.org/
   2012/04/26/151417943/
   checking-in-on-eurozone-economies>. Transcript.

"Ethanol." *Times Topics*. New York Times, 3 Jan. 2012.
   Web. 26 May 2012. <http://topics.nytimes.com/top/
   reference/timestopics/subjects/e/ethanol/index.html>.

"The Ethanol Myth." *Consumer Reports*. Oct. 2006:
   15–19. *EbscoHost*. Web. 28 May 2012.

Hill, Jason, et al. "Climate Change and Health Costs of
   Air Emissions from Biofuels and Gasoline." *Proceedings of the National Academy of Science* 106.6 (2009):
   1077–1082. *PubMed Central*. Web. 6 Apr. 2009.

Pear, Robert. "After Three Decades, Tax Credit for Ethanol Expires." *New York Times*. New York Times, 1
   Jan. 2012. Web. 10 June 2012. <http://www.nytimes
   .com/2012/01/02/business/energy-environment/after-
   three-decades-federal-tax-credit-for-ethanol-expires
   .html?_r=1>.

Piller, Dan. "Oil Companies Say E15 Ethanol Damages
   Engines." *Des Moines Register*. Des Moines Register,
   16 May 2012. Web. 10 June 2012.
   <http://blogs.desmoinesregister.com/dmr/index.php/
   2012/05/16/oil-companies-say-e15-ethanol-damages-
   engines/>.

Rosenoer, Michal. "Celebrating the New Year with a
   Victory Against Corn Ethanol." *Blog: Friends of the
   Earth*. Friends of the Earth, 6 Jan. 2012. Web.
   28 May 2012. <http://www.foe.org/news/blog/
   2012-01-celebrating-the-new-year-with-a-victory-
   against-corn>.

Instructor re-
quires URLs be
included for Web
items. Compare
formats for dif-
ferent types of
sources to mod-
els in Appendix.

When URLs wrap
across lines,
they should
break only at
slash marks.

Inclusive pagi-
nation for print
publication from
library database.
No URLs for da-
tabase citations
because each
search is unique.

Building an MLA Citation

Providing accurate, conventionally formatted documentation of your sources will enhance your own authority as a writer at the same time that it gives your readers essential information for follow-up. This appendix provides model Modern Language Association (MLA) citation formats for both internal citations and lists of works cited. As we discussed in Chapter 6 (pp. 143–144), readers expect the lists of works that you cited in your paper to provide full information about the sources referred to and discussed in your paper. To link the paper's references to sources within your works cited list, use a brief parenthetical in-text citation that contains the word at the left margin of your list, usually the author's last name.

The model formats we offer in this appendix cover the most common types of paper and electronic sources that students use in composition courses; however, it is necessarily brief. If you need to cite a source for which you cannot find an appropriate model here, or if you need advice about how to include additional details, we recommend that you consult one of the following:

1. A handbook recommended specifically for your course, which very likely has format models for a number of different citation systems
2. The current edition of the *MLA Handbook for Writers of Research Papers*. We used the seventh edition (2009), a paper copy of which will almost certainly be available in your library's reference section. In addition, a librarian will probably also have access to an online copy.
3. The online writing centers at Purdue <http://owl.english.purdue.edu/owl/resource/585/01/> and the University of Wisconsin–Madison <http://writing.wisc.edu/Handbook/DocMLA.html>, both of which offer models and advice for citation systems used in a number of disciplines.

Formatting MLA In-Text Citations

The basic skeleton of an MLA in-text or parenthetical citation is simple: author's surname plus, if you are quoting or paraphrasing, the page number where the original material is located:

(Name 00)

Inserting the author's surname this way helps readers find the full citation of the work by scanning the left margin of your alphabetically arranged works cited list. The page number tells them exactly where to find a quote or paraphrased material. Notice that MLA format does not put a comma between the name and the page number.

Quick Guidelines for Placement and Content

1. **Using Natural Breaks.** Place the parenthetical citation as close as possible to the material you are quoting or paraphrasing, at a natural break within the sentence or at the end of the sentence that includes the quotation or paraphrase from the source. All quoted material should be cited immediately at the end of the phrase or sentence in which the quotation appears. Here is a hypothetical example of two citations in one sentence:

   > Romance novels are said to feed unrealistic fantasies (Hopewell 15) because they lack "moral ambiguity" (Gray and Sachs 76).

2. **Including the Citation Within Your Sentence.** Put a space before the first parenthesis and place the sentence-ending period after the second parenthesis.

3. **Working with Attributive Tags.** If the author's name is already in the sentence, you may omit it from the parenthetical citation. For example:

   > Postman and Powers say we need to understand "even the delusions of the television news industry" (27).

4. **Referring to Entire Works.** If you want to write a sentence that refers to an entire work (no specific page numbers), mention the author's name in the sentence, then include full information on your works cited list. Readers will know to find it by looking for the author's name. For some documents, such as a Web site or an annual report, the sponsoring organization or agency—that is, a **corporate author**—can be listed in the parenthetical citation and at the left margin of the list of works cited. These cites might look like this:

   > (Greater Milwaukee Foundation 44)
   > (Centers for Disease Control iii)

5. **Using Short Titles.** If a source lists no author—as is the case for many Web pages—use a shortened form of the work's title in the parenthetical citation. For this short title, use the first word or two from the full title as it will appear at the left margin of the alphabetized works cited list. Use the appropriate title punctuation—quotation marks or italics. The following example cites a paraphrase from an article with no listed author. The writer included the publication title in his sentence to convey its authority, but knew the article title at the left margin would be how readers would find the full citation.

> *Consumer Reports* contended in 2009 that there is no economic
> advantage to buying a flex fuel vehicle ("Ethanol" 16).

In the following example, which refers to an article entitled "Can Anti-oxidants Save Your Life?" the writer needed to use two words for the short title because using just "Can" would seem cryptic:

> ("Can Antioxidants" 5)

Short titles are also useful when you are working with more than one source by the same author. Using citations like this will help a reader know quickly which article you mean:

> (Friedman, "Eastern")
>
> (Friedman, "Paul Simon")

6. **Avoid Using "Anonymous."** Although some library databases label articles with unnamed authors "anonymous," you should not use that word in your citations unless it appears in the actual publication. In the event that you are working with two works with no listed author and the same title—for example, an encyclopedia article and a Web site about jellyfish—MLA recommends that you include a distinguishing element from the full citations to help readers locate the right source on the works cited list, such as

> ("Jellyfish," Britannica)
>
> ("Jellyfish," Sea Science)

Variations

When You Must Quote Indirectly. If you want to use something that one source attributes to another source, it is best to find the original version and cite it directly. Only then can you be assured that the quotation is accurate and that you understand its context. However, if you can't get to the original, refer to it in the sentence itself and put your indirect source in a parenthetical citation that includes the abbreviation "qtd. in"—for "quoted in." For example:

> Robert Hughes says that reading is a collaboration "in which
> your imagination goes halfway to meet the author's" (qtd. in
> MacFarquhar).

When an Article Has Only One Page, or Page Numbers Are Unavailable. MLA format permits omission of page numbers from an in-text citation, even for a quotation, in three circumstances: (1) when an article is published on a Web site without page or paragraph numbers, (2) when a print article is complete on one page, and (3) when a print article has been retrieved from a periodicals database in a format where it is not possible to pinpoint page numbers. In all three cases, if the author's name is already in the sentence, you won't need an additional parenthetical cite. The assumptions here are (a) that readers can find any page number(s) from the full citation, and (b) once they locate the material, they will be able to search electronically to find the quoted words if they wish. Note the differences in these two examples:

> Kathleen Parker responded that the shooting death of six-year-old Kayla Rolland pushed "the limits of rational thought."

> The shooting death of six-year-old Kayla Rolland outraged many people, including a columnist who said it pushed "the limits of rational thought" (Parker).

When a Work Has More Than One Author. For two or three authors, include all their names; for four or more authors, you have the option of using the first author's name plus "et al.," which abbreviates the Latin term for "and others." The term should not be italicized; "al" is followed by a period. MLA format does not include a comma between "al." and the page number. Some examples:

> (Fisher and Rinehart 438)

> (Fisher, Rinehart, and Manber 12)

> (Manber et al. 84)

When Two Authors Have the Same Surname. Use first and last name in any attributive tag, or add the author's first initial to the parenthetical citation:

> Kathryn Schabel writes ... (17).

> (K. Schabel 17)

> Mattias Schabel reports ... (267).

> (M. Schabel 267)

Setting Up an MLA Works Cited List

The important guidelines in this section will help you format your works cited lists accurately and efficiently. The care you take in formatting citations will convey the care with which you have approached your writing project and will thus enhance your credibility. The quality of your list will reflect the quality of your work.

The Basics

1. Your list of sources should begin on a separate page at the end of your paper. Center the title "Works Cited" at the top of the page.

2. Use the format illustrated in Figure A.1, from Jack's paper on corn ethanol, and the model citations provided later in this chapter. Note that the first line of each citation starts at the left margin with any subsequent lines indented a half inch, a format called "**hanging indent**." This format helps readers quickly locate the word(s) provided by in-text citations. If you have trouble setting up the indents, consult your software's help screens.

3. Use double-spacing throughout.

4. Include in this list *all* materials that you refer to in the body of your paper, but *only* those materials.

5. Arrange all citations alphabetically according to the author's last name. If the source lists no author, alphabetize by the title. When alphabetizing, ignore *the*, *a*, and *an* in book and article titles. Alphabetize two or more works by the same author first by the author's name, then by the first words of the title.

Process Advice for Compiling a Works Cited List

1. To avoid omissions and confusion, add citations to your list while you are composing and integrating each source into your paper. This process

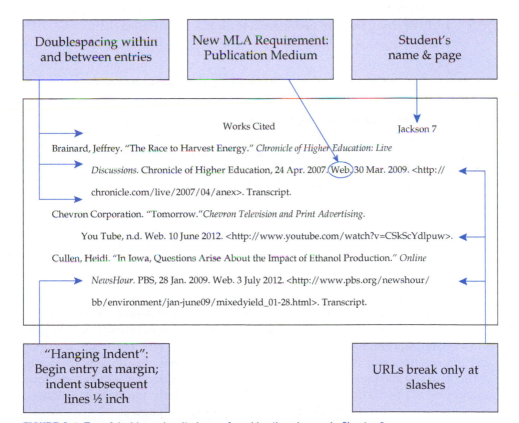

FIGURE A.1 Top of Jack's works cited page from his ethanol paper in Chapter 6

will ensure that you do not omit citations and will allow you to create parenthetical citations that match the left margin of the full citation list. An efficient technique for compiling the list as you write is to keep a separate file open just for the works cited list so that whenever you use outside material in your paper you can immediately add the full information needed for a citation. You can later alphabetize the list and polish the citation format. Just get the full information where you can find it later. Working this way will help you avoid last-minute scrambles to recover missing citation information.

2. As part of final proofreading, take a few minutes to verify that each of your in-text citations matches a full citation on your works cited list. Go from the parenthetical citation to the works cited list just as a reader would. Doing this will reveal any citations missing from your list. Then check in reverse—use your word processor's search function to move from the list back to the in-text citations. This will help you discover whether any in-text citations have been accidentally deleted during revision or whether you have used the wrong word in the parenthetical citation. Unfortunately, an omitted in-text citation can prompt questions from your instructor and be embarrassing. Checking your list against your text will also help you discover any citations that you listed during early drafting that are no longer relevant. Simply delete them.

Model MLA Citation Formats

Readers who are looking at citations want to know four basic pieces of information: who (author), what (title), when (date), and where (*where* it was and can be retrieved—including the publication medium). The details required to fill out these information categories vary according to the type of source you are citing. For example, book citations need to provide information about the publisher (both "who" and "where"), and article citations need to provide specific calendar dates and inclusive page numbers. In addition, MLA style guidelines require information about publication medium, such as "print" or "Web," and many instructors will require that you include the URLs for any materials you use directly on the Web, as you can see in Jack's works cited list at the end of Chapter 6.

Citation formats are designed to present the four key information elements in parallel sequence across all types of materials so that readers can take in content quickly even as they note differences in the types of information provided. The common basic sequence will also help you efficiently pull together the information you need for communicative citations. In the lists of model formats in the next section, we follow the MLA handbook's sequence of four categories: (1) periodical publications (such as scholarly journals, magazines, and newspapers) in print and accessed from library subscription databases, (2) nonperiodical publications in print (books and parts of books), (3) Web publications (including newspaper sites), and (4) other commonly cited materials and media (for example, visual material, sacred texts, and recordings).

Citation Models for Articles in Periodicals

This section presents model citations for articles from print periodicals that you access either from paper copy or through a library subscription service that provides access to an online database such as ProQuest or EbscoHost. Notice that that citations for material retrieved through an online database must include information about print publication even though the publication medium to list regarding your own access is "Web." Retrieve the information about print publication from the article as it appears in the database. If you need to cite a periodical article accessed through a public Web site, including sites sponsored by magazines and newspapers, find an appropriate model in the Web Sources section of this appendix, beginning on page 166.

Figure A.2 illustrates how to arrange the key elements needed to record information about articles retrieved from a printed publication and articles retrieved via library databases. Whereas listing the author and title can be fairly straightforward, providing the publication information involves considerable detail so that your readers can pinpoint the source and judge its reliability as well as follow up for more information as they desire.

Notes About Formatting Article Citations

1. Do not include subtitles of articles unless they are essential to a reader's understanding. (They have often been inserted by editors, not the author, to lure people into reading the text.)
2. If no author is listed, begin with the article title. Do not use the word "anonymous" that appears in some databases unless it appears in print on the article in the periodical.
3. Capitalize all words of a title except *the, a, an,* and short conjunctions and prepositions. Do this even if the words are not capitalized in the original or in the database.
4. Drop the initial *the* from the names of periodicals.
5. For scholarly journals, include volume and issue numbers in all citations. However, these are not needed for general circulation magazines or newspapers.
6. Provide inclusive pages—numbers of the first and last page—whenever possible. If the pages are not consecutive, provide the first page number followed by a plus sign. If the page numbers are not available, use "n. pag."
7. Library databases often provide more information than is required by MLA. For example, you do not need to provide the journal or magazine's

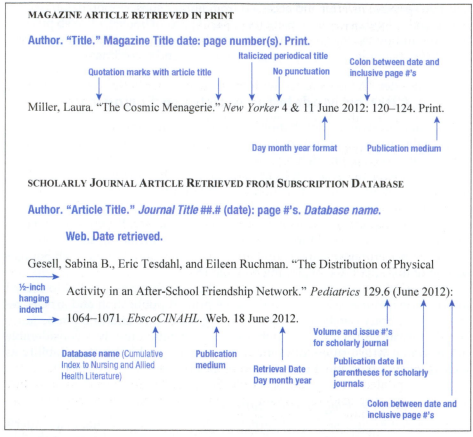

FIGURE A.2 Information elements for MLA-style citations of articles retrieved in print or via online library database

geographic location, and you should not include lengthy names of the database or other versions from the same company.

8. Do not include in your citations the URLs from database searches. They will not help readers because they are unique to each search.

Scholarly Journal Articles by More Than Three Authors

PAPER VERSION

Hansen, Martha, et al. "The Impact of School Daily Schedule on Adolescent Sleep." *Pediatrics* 115.6 (2005): 1555–61. Print.

ELECTRONIC VERSION RETRIEVED THROUGH LIBRARY DATABASE

Hansen, Martha, et al. "The Impact of School Daily Schedule on Adolescent Sleep." *Pediatrics* 115.6 (2005): 1555–61. *EbscoCINAHL*. Web. 19 Apr. 2009.

Magazine and Newsletter Articles

TRADE MAGAZINE ARTICLE ACCESSED VIA PRINT
Brainard, Jeffrey. "The Big Deals in Biofuels." *Chronicle of Higher Education* 20 Apr. 2007: A18. Print.

- The letter "A" is included with the page number in this citation because this weekly publication, like many newspapers, has more than one section, each with separate page numbers.

TRADE MAGAZINE ARTICLE ACCESSED VIA LIBRARY DATABASE
Thevenot, Brian. "Myth-Making in New Orleans." *American Journalism Review* December/January 2006: 30–37. *ProQuest*. Web. 3 Mar. 2011.

GENERAL CIRCULATION MAGAZINE ACCESSED VIA PRINT
Colin, Chris. "Dogs of War." *Smithsonian* July/August 2012: 18. Print.

NEWSLETTER ARTICLE ACCESSED VIA PRINT
"Sweet News About Chocolate." *University of California, Berkeley Wellness Letter* Feb. 2012: 1. Print.

Newspaper Articles

NOTES ABOUT CITING NEWSPAPER ARTICLES
- Newspaper Web sites are not considered periodicals because they are not updated on a regular schedule. See page 169 for format models, but to help your readers access a permanent reference, try to cite these articles via a library database such as *Lexis-Nexis*. To do that accurately, you may need to check the database a few days after you spot the article on the Web.
- Give the paper's name as it appears in the masthead, but omit the introductory *the*.
- If the city is not included in the name, add it in square brackets after the name: e.g., *Times-Picayune* [New Orleans].
- If an edition is listed, include it after the date because different editions of the same day's paper may include different material and pagination.
- If sections of the paper are paginated separately, include identifying letters or labels (e.g., A9 or Sun. mag. 15).

NEWSPAPER ARTICLE ACCESSED VIA PAPER COPY
Stanley, George. "Beat Reporters Bring Depth to Coverage." *Milwaukee Journal Sentinel* 22 Feb. 2009, final metro ed.: A2. Print.

NEWSPAPER ARTICLE ACCESSED VIA LIBRARY DATABASE
Weingarten, Gene. "Doonesbury's War." *Washington Post* 22 Oct. 2006, Sun. mag.: W14+. *Lexis-Nexis Academic*. Web. 12 Feb. 2008.

EDITORIAL OR OPINION PIECE

"The Rights of Female Soldiers." Editorial. *New York Times* 1 June 2012, NY ed.: A26.
Print.

"The Supreme Court's Civics Lesson." Editorial. *Washington Post* 30 March 2012,
Regional ed.: A16. *Lexis-Nexis Academic*. Web. 1 June 2012.

LETTER TO THE EDITOR

- Use the genre label "Letter" after the title, if a title is given. Otherwise,
  use the word "Letter" without italics as a substitute title.
  Drinkwater, Ray. "Questioning College." Letter. *New Yorker* 21 May 2012:
  5. Print.

REVIEW

- After the author and title of the review, include the label "Rev. of," followed by the title of the reviewed work and the name (as relevant) of its
  author, director, performer, or translator with an identifying label. Note
  the comma between the title and "by."

  Delbanco, Andrew. "Her Calling." Rev. of *When I Was a Child, I Read Books*, by
  Marilynne Robinson. *New York Times Book Review* 22 April 2012: BR13. Print.

  Fischer, Mike. "Staples Even More Believable." Rev. of *The Blonde, the Brunette
  and the Vengeful Redhead*, by Robert Hewett, dir. Joseph Hanreddy. *Milwaukee
  Journal Sentinel* 1 June 2012, final ed.: 6B. Print.

- If the review is untitled, the reviewer's name is followed directly by the
  "Rev. of" label, as in the following example:

  Grimm, Nancy Maloney. Rev. of *Between Talk and Teaching: Reconsidering the
  Writing Conference*, by Laurel Johnson Black. *College Composition and Commu-
  nication* 52.1 (2000): 156–59. Print.

- If the review is untitled and unsigned, begin with "Rev. of" and alphabetize the entry under the work's title. The following citation would be
  alphabetized under "J":

  Rev. of *The Jerusalem Syndrome*. *New Yorker* 4 Sept. 2000: 8+. Print.

Citation Models for Books and Other
Nonperiodical Print Sources

Figure A.3 illustrates placement of the information elements needed to cite
books accessed in print: (1) author, (2) title, (3) publication information (place,
publisher name, and date), and (4) publication medium. For most books, the
publication medium would be listed as "Print." But if you work with an electronic copy of a book, you will need instead to use "Web" or, if you retrieved the
book through a digital device, list that file type or simply insert "Digital file."

Book by One Author

Holzer, Harold A. *The Lincoln Anthology: Great Writers on His Life and Legacy from 1860 to
Now*. New York: Library of America, 2008. Print.

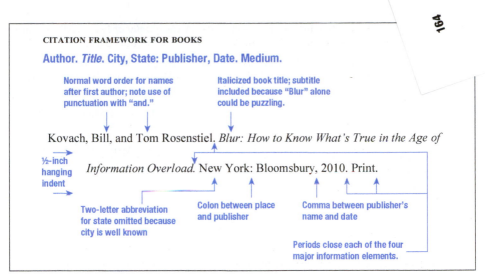

CITATION FRAMEWORK FOR BOOKS

Author. *Title*. City, State: Publisher, Date. Medium.

Normal word order for names after first author; note use of punctuation with "and."

Italicized book title; subtitle included because "Blur" alone could be puzzling.

Kovach, Bill, and Tom Rosenstiel. *Blur: How to Know What's True in the Age of*

½-inch hanging indent

Information Overload. New York: Bloomsbury, 2010. Print.

Two-letter abbreviation for state omitted because city is well known

Colon between place and publisher

Comma between publisher's name and date

Periods close each of the four major information elements.

FIGURE A.3 Information elements for MLA-style citations of books and other nonperiodical work in print

Book with Two or Three Authors

Brooke, Robert, Ruth Mirtz, and Rick Evans. *Small Groups in Writing Workshops: Invitations to a Writer's Life*. Urbana, IL: NCTE, 1994. Print.

Using "et al." for More Than Three Authors

Mabey, Nick, Stephen Hall, Clare Smith, and Sujata Gupta. *Argument in the Greenhouse: The International Economics of Controlling Global Warming*. London: Routledge, 1997. Print.

OR

Mabey, Nick, et al. *Argument in the Greenhouse: The International Economics of Controlling Global Warming*. London: Routledge, 1997. Print.

Edited Collections or Anthologies

Severino, Carol, Juan C. Guerra, and Johnnella E. Butler, eds. *Writing in Multicultural Settings*. New York: MLA, 1997. Print.

Selections from an Edited Collection/Anthology

Present inclusive (i.e., first and last) page numbers for the selection as a separate item between the date and the publication medium.

Christian-Smith, Linda K. "Voices of Resistance: Young Women Readers of Romantic Fiction." *Beyond Silenced Voices: Class, Race, and Gender in U.S. Schools*. Ed. Lois Weis and Michelle Fine. New York: State U of New York P, 1993. 169–89. Print.

Welch, James. "Christmas Comes to Moccasin Flat." *A Geography of Poets*. Ed. Edward
    Field. New York: Bantam, 1979. 43. Print.

If the selection is from a book that collects work by one author, use the same
format. If an editor is listed on the title page, insert the name between the title
and the publication information.

Hribal, C. J. "Consent." *The Clouds in Memphis*. Amherst, MA: U of Massachusetts P,
    2000. 55–67. Print.

Williams, William Carlos. "This Is Just to Say." *Selected Poems*. Ed. Robert Pinsky. New
    York: New American Library, 2004. 78–79. Print.

Books with Corporate Author

Hayward Gallery. *Rhapsodies in Black: Art of the Harlem Renaissance*. Berkeley: U of Cali-
    fornia P, 1997. Print.

Books with No Author or Editor Listed on Title Page

Harvard Business Review on Communicating Effectively. Boston: Harvard Business Review
    Press, 2011. Print.

Strong Hearts: Native American Visions and Voices. New York: Aperture, 1995. Print.

Two or More Works by the Same Author

Alphabetize first by the author's name, then by the works' titles. On the second
and any subsequent entries, instead of the author's name, type three hyphens,
a period, then the title.

Quindlen, Anna. "The Agony of Writing." *Wsj.com*. Wall Street Journal, 20 Apr. 2012.
    Web. 1 June 2012.[1]

---. *How Reading Changed My Life*. New York: Ballantine, 1998. Print.
---. *Lots of Candles, Plenty of Cake*. New York: Random, 2012. Print.
---. *One True Thing*. New York: Random, 1994. Print.

When Titles Include Titles

To indicate that a book title includes the title of another book, omit the italics
on the included title.

Sten, Christopher. *Sounding the Whale:* Moby-Dick *as Epic Novel*. Kent, OH: Kent State
    UP, 1996. Print.

To indicate that a book title includes a short story or essay title, add quotation marks around the shorter title and retain italics for the entire book title.

Dock, Julie Bates, ed. *Charlotte Perkins Gilman's "The Yellow Wall-Paper" and the History of
    Its Publication and Reception: A Critical Edition and Documentary Casebook*. University
    Park, PA: Penn State UP, 1998. Print.

---

[1] For more information about citing material found on the Web page of a newspaper, see the next
section, beginning on page 166.

Introduction, Preface, Foreword, or Afterword of a Book

Hirsch, Edward. Introduction. *Transforming Vision: Writers on Art*. By Art Institute of
   Chicago. Boston: Little, 1994. 9–11. Print.

Cross References

When you cite several works from the same collection, avoid repetition and
save space by using one main entry to which citations for specific works within
it can refer. In the following sample set of cross-references, note that there is no
punctuation between the editor's name and the page numbers.

Stanford, David, ed. *Doonesbury.Com's* The Sandbox: *Dispatches from Troops in Iraq and
   Afghanistan*. Kansas City, MO: Andrews McMeel, 2007. Print.

—. "Editor's Note." Stanford xiii–xv.

Trudeau, G.B. Introduction. Stanford xvii–xviii.

Tupper, Benjamin. "Decency and Honor." Stanford 190–91.

- The short cross-reference citations do not need to include the medium of
  publication.
- In the main citation example above, *The Sandbox* is not italicized within the
  book title because it is the title itself of a Web site.

Selections from a Reference Book

Cite material from reference books as you would work from a collection, but
omit the editor's name.

- If the article is signed, begin with the author's name.
- If contents in the reference book are arranged alphabetically, you may
  omit volume and page from the works cited list citation, but you should
  include them in the parenthetical citation in your text.
- If the reference work is well known and appears in frequent editions, full
  publication information is not needed.
- If you are drawing information from an online or electronic source, see
  page 169.

MATERIAL FROM FAMILIAR SOURCE ARRANGED ALPHABETICALLY
"Rembrandt." *The New Encyclopedia Britannica*. 1998. Print.

SPECIFIC DICTIONARY DEFINITION AMONG SEVERAL
"Story." Def. 9. *Random House Dictionary of the English Language*. 2nd ed. 1987. Print.

Brochures or Pamphlets

Understanding South Asian Art: India. Washington, D.C.: Smithsonian Institution, 1999.
   Paper.

Voices Behind Bars: National Public Radio and Angola State Prison. New York: The Journalism School, Columbia University, [2010]. Paper.

- The date is given in brackets because it is not printed on the pamphlet but is
  listed as the copyright date on an order form.

Formats for Citing Web Sources

Finding and formatting the information required for Web sources may be a little more complex than for periodicals and books, but because Web sources are inherently unstable, they deserve the most attention to detail. Although the publication medium will be obvious (Web), and most reliable sources will include the basic elements used for book and article citations (author, title, and publication information), this information may not be readily evident for many Web sources. In addition, because Web sources are revised frequently and irregularly, a fifth element is required: date of access. Many instructors will ask that you also include the URL, the Uniform Resource Locater. To save space, we do not include URLs in the models, but Jack's paper at the end of Chapter 6 provides models for including them. Check with your instructor to be sure about whether you are expected to include them. The *MLA Handbook*'s official ruling on the inclusion of URLs states that they are needed only when readers "probably cannot locate the source without it or when your instructor requires it" (182).

The annotated citation in Figure A.4 illustrates how to arrange citations for Web sources (including a URL). As you gather information for building these citations, remember that your goal should always be to provide readers with meaningful information and context as well as to allow them to access the same Web site you accessed as efficiently as possible. Missing information may, of course, be a signal that the source is inherently unreliable, but even valuable sources might not include an author for some material. The following formatting notes offer advice about how to manage these problems.

CAUTIONARY NOTE: KNOW YOUR SOURCE

If you do not know the agenda of the people or organization behind a site, you need to consider whether to use the site as a source at all. At the very least, work to verify the information through other sources. In cases where it is difficult to discern the sponsor or publisher of the page, it would be wise to spend a few minutes searching for the information by breaking down the site's URL or doing other detective work. If you cannot determine a sponsor or publisher and still want to use the source, insert the notation "N.p." (for no publisher) in the citation, following the model in Figure A.4.

However, if you cite a source without definite information about who is behind it, you take a great risk in regard to the reliability of the content. One notorious example is a site with the URL <www.martinlutherking.org>, which announces that it is "hosted" by an organization called "Stormfront." A click on the name takes one to Stormfront's Web site, which prominently features the slogan, "White Pride, World Wide." Although the group has a right to post material in accordance with members' beliefs, the notion of "white pride" makes one question the reliability of the information it presents about civil rights leader Rev. Martin Luther King, Jr.

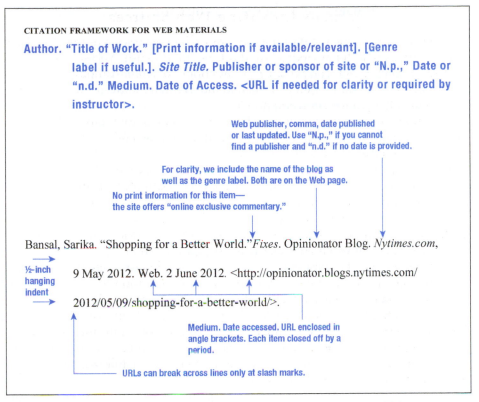

CITATION FRAMEWORK FOR WEB MATERIALS

Author. "Title of Work." [Print information if available/relevant]. [Genre label if useful.]. *Site Title.* **Publisher or sponsor of site or "N.p.," Date or "n.d." Medium. Date of Access. <URL if needed for clarity or required by instructor>.**

Web publisher, comma, date published or last updated. Use "N.p.," if you cannot find a publisher and "n.d." if no date is provided.

For clarity, we include the name of the blog as well as the genre label. Both are on the Web page.

No print information for this item— the site offers "online exclusive commentary."

Bansal, Sarika. "Shopping for a Better World." *Fixes.* Opinionator Blog. *Nytimes.com,*

½-inch hanging indent

9 May 2012. Web. 2 June 2012. <http://opinionator.blogs.nytimes.com/

2012/05/09/shopping-for-a-better-world/>.

Medium. Date accessed. URL enclosed in angle brackets. Each item closed off by a period.

URLs can break across lines only at slash marks.

FIGURE A.4 Information elements for MLA-style citations of works accessed via the Web

Notes About Finding and Formatting Information for Web Materials

1. If a Web site offers citation advice, use the information elements provided, but present them in the MLA format illustrated in the examples that follow. (Not all Web sites will be up to date regarding the latest MLA format.)

2. When you do need to include a URL, follow MLA format by copying the URL from your browser screen and pasting it inside angle brackets at the end of the citation. After the closing angle bracket, add a final period.

3. When you need to break URLs across lines of text, do so only at slash marks (/). Adding any punctuation may lead to errors for someone attempting to follow the URL, and breaking at a hyphen can create confusion: Readers will wonder whether the hyphen is part of the URL.

4. To punctuate the title of a document that is distinct within a Web site, use quotation marks.

5. The title of a Web site should be italicized. It is one of the most important identifiers in the citation. If the site title is not absolutely clear from the screen layout, use the title that appears at the very top of your browser

screen. When no Web site title is immediately apparent, break down the URL to find the larger site.

6. If there is no clear title for a document or site, you could use a genre label such as "Home page" (without quotation marks). Or use the organization's name. The MLA *Handbook* shows an example of a citation that includes the same organizational name in three places: author, site title, and sponsoring organization.

7. Capitalize every word in the title except *a, an, the,* and short conjuctions and prepositions, just as with print publications, even if the words are not capitalized in the original.

8. If the Web page indicates that the work has appeared in print, include that information between the work's title and the site's title, following the models for print versions of the same kind of material (journals, newspapers, etc.).

9. The name of the institution or organization sponsoring the site provides important information about context and reliability. Note in the model citations that the publisher/sponsor item is followed by a comma, before the date of publication or last update. If no publisher/sponsor is available, insert "N.p.," for "no publisher," capitalized and with the comma but without quotation marks.

10. The timeliness of your source is very important. Look for the posting date at the top of an article, near a byline, at the end of the specific work, or at the very bottom of the page. If no date is available, use "n.d." without quotation marks.

12. Your own date of accessing the site is important because Web sites can change rapidly. By including the date you establish your point of reference.

Online Material from Scholarly Journals

ARTICLE FROM WEB SITE OF PRINT-BASED SCHOLARLY JOURNAL

Haynes, Alex B., et al. "A Surgical Safety Checklist to Reduce Morbidity and Mortality in a Global Population." *New England Journal of Medicine* 360.5 (2009): 491–499. *NEJM.org,* n.d. Web. 25 Apr. 2009.

ARTICLE PUBLISHED ONLINE BY A SCHOLARLY JOURNAL
WITHOUT PRINT INFORMATION

Mednick, S., et al. "The Restorative Effect of Naps on Perceptual Deterioration." Advance Online Publication. *Nature Neuroscience.* Salk Institute for Biological Studies, 28 May 2002. Web. 2 Feb. 2009.

ARTICLE FROM A SCHOLARLY E-JOURNAL

Hassebrock, Frank, and Brenda Boyle. "Memory and Narrative: Reading *The Things They Carried* for Psyche and Persona." *Across the Disciplines* 6 (3 Apr. 2009): n. pag. Web. 25 Apr. 2009.

Material from an Online Reference Database

"Kempe, Margery." *Encyclopaedia Britannica Online*. Encyclopedia Britannica, n.d. Web. 25 Apr. 2009.

Online Material from Magazines, Newspapers, and News Sites

ARTICLE FROM WEB SITE OF A PRINT-BASED PERIODICAL,
PRINT DETAILS NOT AVAILABLE

Pecastaing, Camille. "French Socialism, Take Two." *Foreign Affairs*. Council on Foreign Relations, 29 May 2012. Web. 1 June 2012.

ARTICLES FROM NEWSPAPER WEB SITE

Grobart, Sam. "Daddy, What Were Compact Discs?" *nytimes.com*. New York Times, 30 May 2012. Web. 3 June 2012.

"Can We All Get Healthy Together?" Editorial. *Latimes.com*. Los Angeles Times, 28 May 2012. Web. 2 June 2012.

  • Note genre label between the title of the work and the title of the Web site.

ARTICLE FROM AN ONLINE MAGAZINE

Harris, Aisha. "Why Do Ad Agencies Keep Ripping Off Indie Music?" *Slate*. Washington Post Co., 31 May 2012. Web. 1 June 2012.

MATERIAL FROM ONLINE NEWS SITES[2]

Branswell, Helen. "ER's Use of Surgical Checklist Thrill to Research Team Behind Safety Program." *Yahoo! Canada News*. Canadian Press, 14 Mar. 2009. Web. 20 Mar. 2009.

"Tintin Cover Fetches Record-Breaking 1.3m Euros." *BBC News*. British Broadcasting Corporation, 2 June 2012. Web. 2 June 2012.

Material from an Online Information Service

"Guillain-Barré Syndrome." *MedicineNet.Com*. WebMD, n.d. Web. 26 Apr. 2009.

Material Posted to an Organizational Web Site

Pew Research Center. "Journalism, Satire or Just Laughs? 'The Daily Show with Jon Stewart,' Examined." *Journalism.org*. Project for Excellence in Journalism, 8 May 2008. Web. 1 Dec. 2008.

Material from Corporate or Organizational Sites

For the following two examples, because no author was listed, the writer could choose to start the citation with either the company name (as author) or the document title. Because the words at the left margin of the full citation must match the in-text citation, the choice depends on which would make the sentence in the text read better.

---

[2]Online sites that aggregate news from many sources are cited differently from newspaper Web sites because they are not collected in subscription databases.

"From 1903 Until Now." *Harley-Davidson USA*. Harley-Davidson Motor Company, n.d. Web. 3 Apr. 2009.

Trek Bicycle Corporation. "1 World, 2 Wheels: A Trek Commitment." *TrekBikes.com*. Trek Bicycle Corporation, n.d. Web. 15 Oct. 2000.

When a site doesn't offer a title beyond the organization's name, you may use a generic label such as "Home page" (no italics, no quotation marks).

Home page. Committee to Protect Journalists, n.d. Web. 2 June 2012.

Television or Radio Broadcast Available Online

Fosslien, Elisabeth. "How to Get a Job, in Charts and Graphs." Graphics. *Marketplace Money*. American Public Media, 1 June 2012. Web. 2 June 2012.

Morrison, Toni. Interview by Jeffrey Brown. *The NewsHour*. PBS, 29 May 2012. Web. 2 June 2012.

Sound Portraits Productions. "Witness to an Execution." *All Things Considered*. NPR, 12 Oct. 2000. Web. 12 Oct. 2000.

Web-Accessed Visual Materials: Cartoons, Maps, Advertisements, Art

For clarity, insert descriptive or genre labels as needed between the title of the work and the title of the Web page.

Breen, Steve. "Foreign Oil." Cartoon. *2009 Pulitzer Prize-Winning Cartoons*. About.com, 2009. Web. 26 Apr. 2009.

Burundi. Map. *Geneva Foundation for Medical Education and Research*. N.p., n.d. Web. 22 Nov. 2012.

Dove. Advertisement. *Campaign for Real Beauty*. Unilever, 2009. Web. 26 Apr. 2009.

Lawrence, Jacob. *The Migration Series*. Phillips Collection, 2009. Web. 26 Apr. 2009.

Online Postings: Press Releases, Blogs, Tweets

Bartoo, Carole. "Peer Selection After School Can Increase Activity, Reduce Childhood Obesity." Press Release. Vanderbilt University Medical Center, 29 May 2012. Web. 30 May 2012.

Remember to check carefully the reliability of blog and other online postings that you might use as sources. Blogs sponsored by news organizations are more reliable than the blogs of individuals.

Wyss, Jim. "Want Joy? Move to Venezuela." *Blog: Inside South America*. McClatchy Newspapers, 31 May 2012. Web. 2 May 2012.

MLA announced an official format for tweets in March 2012, using as an example this famous tweet that turned out to have been breaking early news of the attack on Osamba bin Ladin's household in 2011. Note that the MLA example uses the following distinct format:

Author Real Name (Username). "Entire tweet." Date, time. Tweet.

Athar, Sohaib (ReallyVirtual). "Helicopter hovering above Abbottabad at 1AM (is a rare event)." 1 May 2011, 3:58 p.m. Tweet.

Citation Formats for Other Materials and Media

Advertisements

Pantene Shampoo. Advertisement. NBC 14 Mar. 2008. Television.

Singapore Airlines. Advertisement. *New Yorker* Feb. 9 & 16, 2009: 37. Print.

Cartoons or Comic Strips

Adams, Scott. "Dilbert." Comic Strip. *Milwaukee Journal Sentinel* 16 Apr. 2009: 2D. Print.

Sacred Texts

Whenever you plan to discuss any sacred texts in a paper, be sure to ask your instructor what kind of citation information you need to provide and what format to use.

Material from the Judeo-Christian Bible as well as from sacred writings in other traditions is typically cited in the text by an abbreviation for the name of the book, then chapter and verse numbers. Page numbers are not used because the citation already permits the reader to find the passage in any version of the Bible. Include the edition of the Bible in your first reference. For example: (*New Oxford Annotated Bible*, Ps. 19:7) refers to this full citation:

New Oxford Annotated Bible. New Revised Standard Version. Ed. Bruce M. Metzger and Roland E. Murphy. New York: Oxford, 1991.

Lecture, Speech, or Conference Paper

Zedillo, Ernesto. "Latin America: Two Hundred Years of Solitude." Walter E. Edge Lecture. Pace Center on Civic Engagement, Princeton University. 5 Mar. 2009.

Video Recordings

Australia's Twilight of the Dreamtime. Writ/Photog. Stanley Breeden. National Geographic Society and WQED, Pittsburgh, 1988. Videocassette.

Sound Recordings

Your decision about whom to cite first—the performer, composer, or conductor—depends on the point you are making. If the original recording date is important, provide it after the title; then indicate the manufacturer and production date followed by the medium of production.

Ma, Yo-Yo, and Bobby McFerrin, perf. "Grace." By Bobby McFerrin. *Hush*. Sony, 1992. CD.

Coltrane, John. Liner notes. *A Love Supreme*. Rec. 9 Dec. 1964. Impulse, 1964. LP.

TV or Radio Programs

"Take This Sabbath Day." *The West Wing*. Writ. Aaron Sorkin. Dir. Thomas Schlamme. NBC. WTMJ, Milwaukee. 9 Feb. 2000. Television.

Works of Visual Art

Lewis, Morris. *Point of Tranquility*. 1959–1960. Acrylic on canvas. Hirshhorn Museum, Smithsonian Institution, Washington, D.C.

Credits

Text Credits

Chapter 1: Imagine you enter a parlor. . . , From" The Philosophy of Literary Form: Studies in Symbolic Action by BURKE, KENNETH Reproduced with permission of UNIVERSITY OF CALIFORNIA PRESS in the format Republish in book via Copyright Clearance Center.; Tony slowly got up from the mat. . . , Excerpt from Kathleen McCormick, The Culture of Reading and the Teaching of English, pages 20–21. Copyright (c) 1994 Reprinted by permission of Manchester University Press.; Illinois Plant Produces Alternate Fuel billboard, Scott Olson/Getty Images; Editorial cartoon by Robert Ariall. 4/22/08, Robert Ariail: © The State/ Dist. By Newspaper Enterprise Association. Inc.; We agree. We need viable alternatives. We're investing millions in geothermal, biofuel and solar technologies, http://www.chevron.com/weagree/?statement=renewables, Chevron Corporation.

Chapter 2: Diagram of Inverted Pyramid Structure Recommended for Organizing Web Content, Used by permission, Kerry Radshaw (www.kerryr.net).; Image of Page One of Research Report from the Scholarly Journal *Appetite*, Reprinted from Appetite, Vol. 57 No. 2, Serge V. Onyper, Timothy L. Carr, John S. Farrar, Brittney R. Ford, "Cognitive advantages of chewing gum. Now you see them, now you don't," p. 327, Copyright (c) 2012, with permission from Elsevier.; Chew On This, Reprinted by permission from The University of California at Berkeley Wellness Letter, February, 2012. www.wellnessletter.com, Regents of the University of California; In summary, the current study. . . (2 lines), Reprinted from Appetite, Vol. 57 No. 2, Serge V. Onyper, Timothy L. Carr, John S. Farrar, Brittney R. Ford, "Cognitive advantages of chewing gum. Now you see them, now you don't," p. 327, Copyright (c) 2012, with permission from Elsevier.; Preparing To Read: Sheri's Process, Gillespie, Paula; Lerner, Neal, Allyn & Bacon Guide To Peer Tutoring, The 1/e. (c) 2000. Reprinted and Electronically reproduced by permission of Pearson Education, Inc., Upper Saddle River, New Jersey.; Physicists' Techniques For Efficient Reading, Academic literacy and the nature of expertise: reading, writing, and knowing in academic philosophy by GEISLER, CHERYL Copyright 1994 Reproduced with permission of TAYLOR & FRANCIS GROUP LLC BOOKS in the format Textbook via Copyright Clearance Center.; Building a Context For Reading, Feldman, Ann Merle, Writing And Learning In The Disciplines, 1st Edition, (c) 1996. Reprinted and Electronically reproduced by permission of Pearson Education, Inc., Upper Saddle River, New Jersey.

Chapter 3: How To Structure A Rhetorical Précis, Based on "The Rhetorical Précis," Rhetoric Review 7; Excerpt from Chap. 6, Monument Wars: Washington, D.C. the National Mall, and the Transformation of the Memorial Landscape by Kirk Savage, (c) 2009 by the Regents of the University of California. Published by the University of California Press. Editorial art drawing by Randy Mack Bishop, by permission of Randy Mack Bishop; Vietnam Veterans Memorial, GOL/Fotolia; "Cover" photo from Milwaukee Urban Ecology Center's Annual Report Web page, Urban Ecology Center; In this combination of two file photos, the Funtime Pier in Seaside Heights, N.J. is shown before and after Superstorm Sandy made landfall on the Jersey Shore.; Top (Mel Evans/AP Images) Bottom (Star Ledger, David Gard/AP Images); Imagine you enter a parlor. . . , From" The Philosophy of Literary Form: Studies in Symbolic Action by BURKE, KENNETH Reproduced with permission of UNIVERSITY OF CALIFORNIA PRESS in the format Republish in book via Copyright Clearance Center.

Chapter 4:   A Lifesaving Checklist, Atul Gawande, "A Lifesaving Checklist" New York Times, Op Ed, December 30, 2007. Copyright (c) 2007. Reprinted by permission of the author.; Peace Corps screen capture, Ready to Make a Difference in 2013?, Courtesy Peace Corps; PAPER because, bringing in the mail is one the few things we still have in common. CNW Group/DOMTAR CORPORATION/ Newscom.

Chapter 5:   Close Up from a Lexis Nexis "Easy Search" Screen Showing Types of Sources Available, Copyright (c) 2012 LexisNexis, a division of Reed Elsevier, Inc. All Rights Reserved. LexisNexis and the Knowledge Burst logo are registered trademarks of Reed Elsevier Properties Inc., and are used with the permission of LexisNexis.; Close Up from a ProQuest Research Library Screen Showing Results of a Search for "financial literacy" AND "teenagers," Showing Alternate Subject Terms, The Screenshot is published with permission of ProQuest LLC. Further reproduction is Prohibited without permission.

Chapter 6:   Dialogue from the online transcript of a NewsHour video, Heidi Cullen, "In Iowa, Questions Arise About the Impact of Ethanol Production" The NewsHour With Jim Lehrer, PBS, January 28, 2009. Copyright (c) 2009 Reprinted by permission of Climate Control.; 2 lines from The Ethanol Myth, "The Ethanol Myth" Copyright 2006 Consumers Union of the US, Inc., Yonkers, NY 10703 1057, a non profit organization. Excerpted with permission from the October 2006 issue of Consumer Reports (R) for educational purposes only. www.ConsumerReports.org.

Photo Credits

11: Whitehouse; **13:** Scott Olson/Getty Images; **14:** Robert Ariail © 2008 The State. Reprinted with permission of UNIVERSAL UCLICK. All rights reserved; **24:** Reprinted by permission from The University of California at Berkeley Wellness Letter, February, 2012. www.wellnessletter.com; **44:** GOL/Fotolia; **45:** Library of Congress, Prints and Photographs Division, Vietnam Veterans Memorial Fund Slide Collection, LC-DIG-ppmsca-05608; **51:** Top (Mel Evans/AP Images); **51:** Bottom (Star-Ledger, David Gard/AP Images); **53:** Randy Mack Bishop; **80:** DOONESBURY © G.B. Trudeau. Reprinted with permission of UNIVERSAL UCLICK. All rights reserved; **87:** Courtesy Peace Corps; **89:** CNW Group/DOMTAR CORPORATION/ Newscom; **90:** CNW Group/DOMTAR CORPORATION/Newscom.

Index